MW00962237

AuthorHouse™
1663 Liberty Drive
Bloomington, IN 47403
www.authorhouse.com
Phone: 1-800-839-8640

© 2014 Philip and Rhonda Wilson. All rights reserved.

No part of this book may be reproduced, stored in a retrieval system, or transmitted by any means without the written permission of the author.

Bible Scriptures from the New International Version (NIV) translation

Published by AuthorHouse 01/10/2014

ISBN: 9781496012227

Library of Congress Control Number: Pending

Any people depicted in stock imagery provided by Thinkstock are models, and such images are being used for illustrative purposes only. Certain stock imagery © Thinkstock.

This book is printed on acid-free paper.

Because of the dynamic nature of the Internet, any web addresses or links contained in this book may have changed since publication and may no longer be valid. The views expressed in this work are solely those of the author and do not necessarily reflect the views of the publisher, and the publisher hereby disclaims any responsibility for them

authorHOUSE®

FINDING PEACE IN
LIFE'S
STORMS

Unshakable Faith for
Uncertain Times

Philip and Rhonda Wilson

Contents

Who Are the Authors?   1

Is God in Control?   4

Is God in Control?   7

The Great Change Agent   11

Thump in the Night   14

Redefining Abundant Life   16

Difficult Days at the Mayo Clinic   18

This Valley Belongs to Praise   20

Team Wilson   24

Remember God's Past Faithfulness   26

Today is Tuesday   30

Pressing Forward without Understanding   34

Date Night   40

My War Within   43

My War Within   46

The Sin of Worry   49

Seven Years After the Stroke   53

Was It God's Will that Our Daughter was Electrocuted?   57

Prayer, the First Line of Defense   72

Beyond Human Limitations   77

The Word "Christian" is an Adjective, Not a Noun   81

More Help Moving Past "Why"   84

How to Help Others Going through a Storm   90

Helping Children through the Storm   95

Is Your Name in the Book of Remembrance?   99

Who Are the Authors?

LIFE BRINGS TRIALS, disappointments, uncertainties, and brokenness. Learning how to handle life's troubles is one of our great human challenges. At some point everyone experiences difficult times. If you have not, just wait—they are coming.

Philip, Rhonda, Matthew, and Caroline Wilson have had their share of struggles in recent years. We are not saying we are special because of this, or that we desire attention; there are plenty of others who have been tested more than we have.

Our goal in writing this book is to glorify God by allowing our story to be a testimony of God's peace in the midst of the storms. We hope it brings deep healing to your soul, as it has to us in writing this book.

How to deal with storms is not only a helpful topic for us but an important topic for Christians to witness their faith to the world. Others watch how you handle problems. Every day you pass people who do not believe how God could exist in such an evil world. We see people every day who have been broken by storms and given up on their faith. You may be their only link to God. Show them your life is different. Showing them how you handle storms is your life sermon.

The Bible gives us many examples of people who have struggled. Consider this passage from 2 Corinthians 11:23–28:

> Are they servants of Christ? (I am out of my mind to talk like this.) I am more. I have worked much harder, been in prison more frequently, been flogged more severely, and been exposed to death again and again. Five times I received from the Jews the forty lashes minus one. Three times I was beaten with rods, once I was pelted with stones, three times I was shipwrecked, I spent a night and a day in the open sea, I have been constantly on the move. I have been in danger from rivers, in danger from bandits, in danger from my fellow Jews, in danger from Gentiles; in

danger in the city, in danger in the country, in danger at sea; and in danger from false believers. I have labored and toiled and have often gone without sleep; I have known hunger and thirst and have often gone without food; I have been cold and naked. Besides everything else, I face daily the pressure of my concern for all the churches.

Do you know who wrote these verses? You might be surprised to know it was Paul, the same Paul who wrote one-third of the New Testament, more of it than anyone else. Paul is considered by most in the Christian church to be the most significant and influential Christian after the resurrection of Jesus.

Is it not interesting that his life was filled with difficulty? You would think someone so significant and so influential would have had an easier life. I would think God would reward someone so important by keeping him away from so many storms.

Rhonda and I have been Christians for more than forty years. Rhonda is the daughter of a Baptist minister. She grew up in a family that "planted" churches. This means they started churches in areas that did not have a church presence. Rhonda had deep spiritual maturity at a young age. My father was also a Baptist minister. When I was growing up, if the church doors were open, we were there. Church was my life! I accepted Christ at a young age and grew to understand what was expected of the Christian life.

Rhonda and I have raised our children in the same way we were raised. We are active in our church, and we strive every day to be good citizens in our community and to be of service to others.

I remember memorizing John 3:16 and being taught how to live the Christian life. The stories I learned as a child were of Daniel in the lion's den, David and Goliath and Moses parting the Red Sea. Stories of victory and God's power! However, I don't remember learning that the Christian life would be hard and filled with tribulations.

Our family was completely turned upside down beginning in 2005. This was the year that, at age thirty-nine, I had a massive stroke. A few years later, in 2012, our six-year-old daughter, Caroline, was electrocuted.

Many of the chapters in this book were originally posts from a blog that was written to update our friends on our medical status during that time. We reorganized the posts into chapters to tell our story and share how our life experiences have helped us understand the answers to the questions: Is God really in control? If so, why do we suffer?

We hope our story will show you how God has encouraged us through our storms, and how He can comfort and encourage you as well. Rhonda wrote some of the chapters and I (Philip) wrote some, and yet others were written by both of us. Use this book to help you move through the storms of life and to the glory of God. God does not want you to go through life alone. You were never meant to live apart from the sustaining help of God. He offers Himself as a guide through life's storms.

Is God in Control?

Philip Wilson

When you accept the fact that sometimes seasons are dry and times are hard and that God is in control of both, you will discover a sense of divine refuge, because the hope then is in God and not in yourself.
Charles Swindoll

I AM REMINDED OF HOW Christians like to say, "God is good all the time." When bad things happen to us, God either causes the bad things or allows them in our life. If God causes or allows bad things to happen, how can this be being good all the time? What could possibly be good when a drunk driver kills a wife and mother or a child dies of cancer? Why do we go through such pain? If God is in control, then why does He not change things in our favor?

Early in my life, I learned that God's plan for delivering us from a storm is greater than our need for relief from the storm. People talk about high school and college, and especially the college years, as "the best days of your life." I understand why they would say that. A roof over your head and little worry about bills—freedom! However, my school days were difficult for me. I am sure others had it worse, but I felt like I was forced to deal with some serious problems in my life before I was ready to, and that made me very angry.

When I was a teenager, I was diagnosed with rheumatoid arthritis. I did not really know what that meant, but shortly after the diagnosis, I saw a commercial on TV for the Juvenile Rheumatoid Arthritis Association of America. The commercial showed a pitiful-looking child in a wheelchair as the announcer said, "Did you know the majority of people confined to wheelchairs are kids under the age of eighteen?" I was tormented with questions: Will I spend my life in a wheelchair? Will I be able to get married and have kids? Who would even marry someone in a wheelchair?

I was angry. This was not fair. For several years I struggled with this condition and its effects on my body. Joints would swell up like balloons—red, inflamed, and very painful. The condition would come on very suddenly, without warning. I remember while in college waking up the morning of a math test and discovering that my feet were so swollen that I could not put on my shoes. I lived off-campus. Our parking was about a half mile from the classroom building. Even if someone dropped me off in front of my building, I could not walk. I just stayed in bed and scored a zero on my test.

I was so prepared and confident for the test. Zeros are not very good for your grade-point average. I tried to obtain an excused absence, but since the condition frequently kept me out of the classroom, I was encouraged to drop out of school until I was physically more able. The teachers did not accept my condition as excusable; instead, they threatened me with probation because of my low GPA. If I did not increase my grade-point average I would be put on academic probation.

Why does God allow this kind of pain? Where is God during times of great struggle? If God loves us, why does He not shield us from storms? When I went to college, for the first time, I had a choice to go to church. I did not go. I did not want to. I once was so involved, but at that time it did not seem that church was useful or beneficial to me. Was that the reason this was happening to me? I was still very angry about my circumstances, because I did not understand why God would let me suffer.

Looking back on those days, I see how my school days changed me. My experience in high school and college shaped me for my adult life. I eventually dealt with my anger and began to look upward to God again. I felt a passion to work with youth, to help them with their teenage struggles. I believed my experiences would help me make a difference in their lives. I understood very well the painful period of being a teenager. I taught eleventh-grade Sunday school and coached the high school church basketball team for a number of years. The youth became my life. I went to their football games and had them over to my house to watch movies. I called them during the week to see what was going on in their lives. All my time was spent working (building my business) and helping youth. I did not have a social life, but it did not really bother me, because I felt I was right where I was supposed to be. After years of teaching and coaching, I met a girl. She was hired by the church I was teaching at to be an assistant to the youth director. She also had a passion to work with youth. We became friends, speaking and meeting often to discuss the youth and planning activities for them. Her name was Rhonda Reed, and she became my wife.

So here is the recap of events.

Because of the struggles in my teenage years, I used those experiences to serve others. This directly led to meeting my future wife. If I had not struggled in my teenage years, I most likely would not have been helping teenagers. Therefore, I never would have met my wife, the most significant person in my life.

Maybe God really is in charge and wants to bless me. He just does not do it in a way, I think it should be done or when I think it should be done.

Is God in Control?

Rhonda Wilson

You must make a decision that you are going to move on. It won't happen automatically. You will have to rise up and say, "I don't care how hard this is, I don't care how disappointed I am, I'm not going to let this get the best of me. I'm moving on with my life.

Joel Osteen

EARLIER IN MY LIFE, I learned God's plan for delivering me from a storm is greater than my need for relief from the storm. As I neared the end of my college days, I struggled to look to the future with confidence. It started with breaking up with my college sweetheart. We had dated for two years and were headed to the altar, but dreams came crashing down with the knowledge we both knew we were not God's best for each other. It still hurt! I felt insecure.

After graduation I decided to live in Birmingham, Alabama, where my college was located. My parents were missionaries and moved around. I felt I had no "home" to go back to. Alone in Birmingham, I began looking for a job and a place to live. I was determined to make it on my own. It was a scary time for me. I had little support or encouragement. All my college friends moved back home, and I did not have a boyfriend. I found a part-time job as an assistant music director for a local church. I lived with a Christian family I knew in Birmingham while continuing to look for full-time work. I helped take care of their kids. In time, this family became my substitute family; they loved me and encouraged me.

I got a full-time job as an assistant to the youth director at a local Baptist church. Both church jobs kept me very busy. I did not have much of a social life, but it didn't matter to me.

I dated casually, and one day met what looked like a "keeper." The first few weeks he treated me like a queen. He seemed to suggest a future for us. I was not sure if he was the one, but I wanted to find out.

And then it happened. One night he took advantage of me. I said "no" but he did not stop. I tried to get away but could not. I trusted him but now he seemed like a monster. I felt shame and guilt. I know it sounds silly, but I felt it was my fault. I did not tell anyone what happened. It was my secret. No one knew that behind the mask of smiles, I was in the pit of despair. But He knew . . .

How could I trust again? If I ever found Mr. Right, would he understand? I felt dirty. I knew in my heart it was not my fault, but I was still overtaken by guilt. My heart hurt and loneliness choked the breath of life from my soul. I missed my family and friends even more and was angry toward God.

I thought I was living God's will. I thought I was a "good Christian girl." I wanted to be "pure" for marriage but now felt contaminated. I thought I was doing the right things and living by His Word. So why did God allow this to happen to me? What did I do to deserve this? Did He not care about my pain?

What a struggle it was to get up in the morning. All I ever wanted to do was have a life that pleased God. Now I struggled just to get out of bed. I somehow managed to keep going.

One of my responsibilities at the church was to assist in planning for the youth's activities. I often spoke with the Sunday school leaders planning activities for the kids. Most of the leaders were several years older than me, but there was one leader just a few years out of college. He was by far the youngest of any of the teachers, just a few years older than the church youth.

He was a businessman and very passionate about the kids. I loved his heart and seeing how he was able to relate to the youth. They loved him, too! My boss loved him and involved him in just about every aspect of the youth ministry.

We became friends. He was serious but very funny, and I was attracted to his dry sense of humor. Slowly, the walls of distrust of men started to come down. I started to feel safe again when I was around him.

Our friendship grew. We talked often on the phone. He was a volunteer for most of the youth activities, and we saw each other several times a week. Every now and then we went out at night to dinner or a movie, sometimes alone and sometimes with others. I started to have feelings for him but did not show them. I was still very fearful of being hurt. I wondered if he felt the same way. We were not romantic but both of us seemed to really enjoy each other's company. How I wanted to love again!

One night it happened. He played in an adult basketball league and He came to pick me up to go to one of his games. Before we left he told me he wanted to talk to me for a minute. He laid it out for me. "I really like you; I cannot tell if it is mutual. You seem very distant sometimes. If it is mutual, tell me. How do you feel about me?"

The walls came down. I told him the feeling was mutual. My future husband kissed me for the first time. I will never forget that first kiss. After that kiss everything changed.

I felt safe again. Soon I told him my secret. He threw his arms around me and said, "I am so sorry. You did not do anything wrong to deserve this." I knew that was true in my heart, but I still needed to hear it. I was once afraid that knowing about what I suffered would cause others to look down on me. Philip said he respected me even more for going through what I went through and not giving up. He seemed to understand my pain and how hard it is sometimes just to get out of bed and put one foot in front of the other. How I wrestled and wrestled with writing this chapter of the book! I didn't want to lay bare the shame I felt. So it is in this wrestling that I tell you, my reader, God's freedom from storms can be found in His saving grace. Is He in control? I believe that He is and can use the storms of our lives to His glory.

We just have to allow Him. I hope in telling my story, it will encourage others who have traveled a similar road.

It is in His grace and mercy that we can rise up as victors. God brought me through the storm and changed me in the process. My storm brought Philip and I together. I am not sure we would have ended up together had I not been through the storm. I don't know that I would have fully appreciated him. He is different from the guys I dated in college. My storm showed me how we could be partners and build a life together using all the hardships for His glory.

The Great Change Agent

Philip Wilson

When one door closes, another opens; but we often look so long and so regretfully upon the closed door that we do not see the one that has opened for us.

Alexander Graham Bell

DOES GOD REALLY TAKE CARE of you in times of trouble? If so, then why are there times He seems so distant when we need Him most? If God loves us, why doesn't He remove the storms from our lives?

David was described as a "man after God's own heart." The Bible does not describe many people like this. Yet David wrote, "Why do you hide your face? Why do you forget our affliction and oppression?"
(Psalm 44:24).

Not everything in our lives is good. Not everything that happens to us is meant for our immediate benefit. The Bible promises that everything, even those things not meant for good, will eventually be worked out for good, in God's plan. Everything that happens to us will fit into His plan, and His plan is for our benefit.

God's specialty is working it out for us. He is the great change agent. Everything that happens in your life is permitted for God's purpose. Unfortunately, we just cannot see it when our circumstances take over. God's ultimate goal for us is character, not comfort. Our character comes from circumstances. Our comfort is not a priority in God's plan for us.

Consider the example of Hezekiah. In 2 Chronicles 32:31, we read, "And so in the matter of the envoys of the princes of Babylon, who had been sent to him to inquire about the sign that had been done in the land, God left him to himself, in order to test him and to know all that was in his heart."

God left Hezekiah alone to test him. God tests us to see how we act when we don't see Him around. He is always there, but we may not feel His presence. Our purpose while here on Earth is to glorify God. He is most pleased by how we act in our storms. The deepest level of glory we can bring to God is praise and thankfulness during trials. This shows we know how to trust God. We know He is in control and working on our behalf in the midst of storms, even though He is not always visible.

Marathoners talk about "the wall." This is the point at which the body shuts down, around mile eighteen. Yet a marathon is twenty-six miles. To finish, you have to deny the pain of the wall and push through to the finish.

God expects us to work through our pain. To finish you have to press on. Moses spent forty years in the wilderness before he encountered the burning bush. God showed up, changing his life. Moses went from a murderer, hiding out in the desert, to the leader chosen to bring God's people (the Israelites) out of slavery. The Bible does not say it, but you get the feeling it took forty years for God to get Moses ready to lead the Israelites. God shows up when we least expect it and changes things.

Let your mess become your message. Let your trials become your testimony. Do not waste the tough times; stay faithful. Keep on doing and praying and remaining in faith, doing what you are supposed to do, and God will show up and take your ordinary life and do extraordinary things. A marathoner's body gives out, and yet he or she continues another seven or eight miles to the finish. Give God the opportunity to bring glory from your pain. That opportunity is there only when we press on, while waiting on God. Unfortunately, we often do not see our victories because we give up before they happen.

In Romans 5:3–5, we learn a little more about the process of God transforming us when we face storms. We read: "Not only so, but we also glory in our sufferings, because we know that suffering produces perseverance; perseverance, character; and character, hope. And hope does not put us to shame, because God's love has been poured out into our hearts through the Holy Spirit, who has been given to us.

Thank God for His presence in the storms. Thank Him for what you have. Thank Him for who He is, for what He has done, and what He will do. Thank Him for being the great "change agent." He is the great "I am." He is sovereign and in control. He is worthy of our praise. Pray that your tough times will not be wasted.

Stay in faith. Our faith grows through resistance. It is like what happens to your muscles when you lift weights. Our faith grows by exercising it. Believe God is in control and is always working His plan for us. God will not allow a storm without having an intended purpose in our life. We serve a big God. He is not limited by our problems. We limit Him. God is more interested in changing you through your storms than in removing your storms. Have faith in the great change agent.

Thump in the Night

Rhonda Wilson

The absence of life's storms does not mean peace, but the presence of God does.
Joyce Meyer

THE DAY STARTED OUT as any other day for us, with Philip at work and Matthew and I playing at home and running errands. As the day progressed, I noticed when talking to Philip, that he was not himself and encouraged him to see a doctor.

Since Philip had had such a hard day, I made his favorite meal, hoping it would encourage him. But his dinner was not going down as it should. He was constantly choking and coughing. Instead of finishing the meal, he went to bed to rest. Later that evening I went to bed and prayed over Philip for God's protection. I did not sleep well; I was listening to his breathing. Something didn't seem quite right.

Thump! My eyes flew open. What is it? Frantically I stumbled out of bed to find Philip on the floor. Oh dear God, is he breathing? My heart was pounding so loudly I thought the neighbors could hear it.

On the way to the hospital I thought about my life as a homemaker and being able to take care of our son and soon-to-be daughter, as I was seven months pregnant. I wondered how our son Matthew would feel when he woke up and I was not there.

A CAT scan confirmed our worst nightmare: Philip had suffered a brainstem stroke. He was in bad shape. I don't know if he knew it at the time, but no one could understand his speech. All his words were undecipherable to the listener. The left side of his body was paralyzed and would require extensive therapy. The right side of his body was partially paralyzed. It was disheartening to see Philip this way.

After a few days in intensive care, we went to see a well-known stroke specialist at the Mayo Clinic in Minneapolis. On the medical jet flight to the clinic, I was comforted that my husband was alive, but I was afraid of the unknown. I am a planner and like to know in advance what to expect. I think for the first time in my life, I had absolutely no clue what was to come. I felt God's presence as I pondered: Will I need to go back to work? How will I take care of Philip? Will he ever walk or talk again? Do we have enough money for Philip's care? Where do we go from here?

I was overwhelmed but still, somehow, had a feeling of peace. I felt like God was looking over me. I was concerned, uncertain, but not feeling defeated.

Redefining Abundant Life

Philip Wilson

It's not that life has been easy, perfect, or exactly as I expected. I just choose to be happy and grateful no matter how it turns out!

Unknown

WE HAVE ALL HAD EXPERIENCES of God changing things. In those moments, we do not see God working, but He is. And yet, still remain those unanswered questions: Why are we tested to trust God during life's storms?

The Bible offers two descriptions of the Christian life. In Jeremiah 29:11, we read, "For I know the plans I have for you, declares the Lord, plans for welfare and not for evil, to give you a future and a hope." And John 10:10 tells us, "The thief comes only to steal and kill and destroy. I came that they may have life and have it abundantly."

The Bible seems to promise good things for us, yet it hints at the trials we will face. What is the relationship between abundant life and trials? This word "abundance" in Greek means "a quantity that is considerably more than what one would expect or anticipate." That sounds pretty good. Jesus promises us a life far better than we could ever imagine.

It is easy for me to visualize what my life would look like if it were "more than what one would expect." It would involve many things, but not suffering. It would be a life of more certainty, less pain, and fewer unknowns. *Could it be that God's vision of abundant life and what it means for us and our vision of abundant life and what God wants for us are not the same?*

God's vision of abundant life is eternal; our vision is temporal, involving much more of this world. For example, do we appreciate the privilege of talking to God through prayer as much as the excitement for that new car? Do we get really excited about our salvation through Christ, or at least as excited as when we buy a new house? We need to get our vision of abundant life more in line with God's. The focus then is not on this world and the things in it we think will make us happy; it is on God.

At the end of the day, if someone asks you, "Did you have a good day today?" does your answer focus on all the things that went wrong and who did what to you? Do you focus on all the things that did not work out as you wanted?

Our focus should be on the eternal, not the temporal. Our lives revolve way too much around this world's issues, such as obtaining money, getting to baseball practice on time, and deciding what's for dinner. The more we interpret the events in our lives with an eternal meaning, the more abundant our lives will be. Interpreting life with an eternal significance is what makes the Christian life make sense for us. We suffer because we are selfish and need help focusing on the eternal. Our ability to have the abundant life God promises directly follows how well we focus on the eternal, because through that focus we glorify God and we find our true purpose.

Difficult Days at the Mayo Clinic

Rhonda Wilson

God will not permit any troubles to come upon us, unless He has a specific plan by which great blessing can come out of the difficulty.
Peter Marshall

DURING THE FIRST FEW DAYS at the Mayo Clinic, the doctors discussed Philip's care recommendations. Up to this point Philip had been put through a series of tests to establish the cause of the stroke. They said he would need six months of therapy for him to be functional enough to go home.

Philip had already lost a significant amount of weight and was unable to swallow food or liquids. The doctors and staff were concerned and felt he could not remain on the feeding tube for the six-month stay. They recommended a PEG tube, which requires a hole cut in the stomach that allows a feeding tube to be inserted directly into the stomach.

What else could we do? I did not want to do the PEG tube. I asked the doctors questions: "Will he ever be able to eat and drink again? How many calories and how much water does he need every day?" The doctors responded, "He won't be able to eat and drink what he needs to. He can't swallow."

I told them I did not want to cut a hole in his stomach and I would make sure he ate what he needed to. The doctors left frustrated.

Our first meal took a little over an hour to finish. I know what it feels like when food "goes down the wrong way." Imagine every other bite of a meal going down the wrong way. Food would go to his lungs and cause him to cough uncontrollably. I would feed him a bite, wait for him to stop coughing, and then give him another bite. Eventually, we finished his meal.

I used "thickener," which when applied to food or drink turns it into a solid. This was the only way he could swallow anything. I was amazed at his composure during meals. He never complained, he never showed anger, and he did not even talk about how much his throat was burning. I know he was in pain. He was gracious and constantly thanking me for my help.

To drink water, he actually had to eat it like Jell-O. Liquids could go straight to his lungs, which would eventually cause pneumonia. So, I thickened his water and fed it to him. He joked, "Mmm, good. I have never eaten water before. This is a new experience."

At night, I lay exhausted emotionally and physically. My mind wandered to thoughts of our son. How lonely he must have felt to not have seen us before we left to go to the hospital. Why is God putting us through all this? What is His purpose? How would this bring glory to God? I knew His ways were not my ways, but everything looked so bleak.

The Bible teaches us to focus on "things above;" I tried, but could not get past the fear that was surrounding us. I told myself, *You must have faith, God is in control.* I actually felt at peace. Not the peace that is an absence of strife, but confidence that the storms would not overcome me. I had confidence that my future, even though unknown, would work out in the end. I knew we needed to just press on and have faith that God was leading our steps. I tried to focus on Him as I drifted off to sleep.

This Valley Belongs to Praise

Philip Wilson

Every human activity, except sin, can be done for God's pleasure, if you do it with an attitude of praise. Rick Warren

HEBREWS 11:1 STATES, "NOW FAITH is confidence in what we hope for and assurance about what we do not see." Understanding what faith is must be important to believers, since the Bible tells us we cannot please God without faith.

Is faith believing something that is not so, or is it positive thinking? Do we just have to convince ourselves of something happening before praying to have our prayers come true? If you pray for a sick person to be healed but he or she dies anyway, did you not truly believe?

Faith is not just hope. It is hope tied to a promise. Without a promise backing our faith, it is just hope. Christian faith is confidence in the promises of God, confidence that His promises will come true.

Living by faith does not mean that if we just believe, God will act. *Living by faith means living as if God will keep his promises.* It is a forward-looking life, anticipating how God will act. There seems to be a relationship between successful living and faith. The happiest people in the world seem to be able to draw on their inner peace, and have mastered the art of living in faith. They seem to know how to draw on God's strength during the storms of life.

In the Bible, Paul talked about "living in contentment." Happy people are content despite their circumstances. Their joy comes from within, because God is the center of their lives. Happy people wake up each morning celebrating where they have come from, and where they are going. Thankfulness increases their happiness. It is not that happy people are thankful; it is that thankful people are happy.

If you asked most people what they want out of life, most would probably say something about peace. People wish they were less anxious about the future, less stressed, and overall more content with their life. They wish they could have more peace, worrying less about how they are going to deal with their storms.

How do you visualize peace? Is it when everything is comfortable and in perfect order? The type of peace mentioned in the Bible is spiritual peace. It is peace that operates in the middle of a storm, not peace created from the absence of storms.

In Isaiah 41:10 we read, "So do not fear, for I am with you; do not be dismayed, for I am your God. I will strengthen you and help you; I will uphold you with my righteous right hand."

Our peace comes from God's presence in the storm, not from God preventing the storm. Understand the difference between world peace and spiritual peace. The world's version of peace is everything going your way, but it leaves the second it sees trouble. Spiritual peace works for both good times and storms.

Do you have spiritual peace? I find that many people would answer, "Not very often." If we are created in God's image, He is in us. We have the characteristics of God in us. One characteristic is peace. No need to pray for peace; we have it already. We just need to make sure our circumstances do not interfere with our peace.

There are several ways to maintain our peace:
- Pay attention to what we are thinking about.
- Understand human motivation.
- Slow down.
- See life as a self-fulfilling prophecy.
- Live a life of praise.

One way to make sure life does not interfere with our peace is to notice what we are thinking about. Are we captive to our thoughts, or are we in control of them? Business books talk about the idea that we move toward what we think about. In sports we talk about winning or losing in your mind, before ever playing the game. What do you think about? Do you complain about what is wrong in your life or focus on what is right? If we want to maintain peace, we cannot dwell on the negative. Peaceful people are positive people.

Did you know you can choose to be happy? Happiness is a choice, not a feeling. It is a choice to focus on God and not your circumstances. When you focus on your circumstances, they dictate your happiness. When you complain about what has happened to you, you never make your life better. You have to choose to be happy, and choose to live every day happy.

People who are able to maintain their peace understand human motivation. They know how to motivate themselves in positive ways that keep them moving forward. We are usually motivated by fear of loss or desire for gain.

For example, do you smoke? Most people who are successful in quitting are lured by the desire for a healthy lifestyle, not by fear of lung cancer. Quitting smoking because you do not want to get cancer usually does not work that well. We are not motivated as successfully by avoiding a negative result as we are by achieving a positive result. It is difficult to turn a negative thought into a positive action. It is hard to live your life trying not to do something.

Another example: if you want to lose weight and need to eat less, it is far more effective to motivate yourself by the desire to look better than by the desire to not look bad. Peaceful people are able to move forward to something desired. Motivation to move forward during a storm helps us create the peace we desire. We don't first receive peace and then move forward. It is somewhat of a "fake it until you make it." When we focus forward in faith, we actually gain peace. People who are able to maintain their peace know when and how to slow down. Many times we pray for God to give us peace when all we really need to do is slow down. Ridiculous schedules and too many obligations create more stress. Most of us don't know how to prioritize and say no to certain people or activities. We must learn to stay still long enough for God to lead us. It is difficult for God to lead busy people who cannot sit still long enough to.

People who are able to maintain their peace understand that life is a self-fulfilling prophecy. You usually get what you expect. Do you know someone who gets sick every year and says over and over, "About this time I always get the flu?" Just like clockwork, every year they get sick, as if germs were looking at the calendar, lurking outside their window, waiting to pounce at the predetermined time.

Positive people seem to talk themselves out of being sick. For Christians, a positive expectancy comes from being a child of God and knowing their position in Christ. They expect God's favor in their life and can't wait to see how God works, especially during storms. They expect to bring God glory. They see themselves as God sees them. As a result, it is easier for them to trust God and press forward during hard times.

Christians who are able to maintain their peace have lives rich in thankfulness. God does not need our praise, but we need to give it. He is glorified when we do. Instead of rising every day with the weight of the world on your shoulders, focus your thoughts on God. Gratitude and praise keeps our focus upward not inward. Problems have of a way of shrinking when we don't focus on them. We are thankful for what God has provided and what He *will* provide in the future. We have peace and contentment in our circumstances because God is in control.

Many people reading this book may be stuck, still mourning over what was lost. They are unhappy and bitter toward God. How sad it is to see someone going through life trying to make everyone around them pay them back for their pain. Stop mourning for what was lost. Forgive those that hurt you.

Remember, forgiveness is for you, not them. Live life for today and have a positive anticipation of the afuture. Praise God. Thank Him for being the great change agent. Life brings mountains and valleys, good times and tough times. I choose to give my valleys to God, and I praise Him every step of the journey.

23

Team Wilson

Rhonda Wilson

It takes a village to raise a child.
Unknown

AFTER A WEEK IN THE intensive care unit at the Mayo Clinic, Philip and I moved to the in-patient rehabilitation floor for therapy. This meant we were a little closer to going home.

Philip had to relearn how to speak, swallow, walk, and move his arms and legs. He was mentally tired and unable to think clearly. Rehabilitation was a grueling six or seven hours a day, six days a week. It tired me out just watching him. Philip amazed me with his physical and mental endurance. He was in better shape than I'd thought. He told me rehabilitation was the closest he would ever come to military boot camp.

My sister-in-law made the trip to the Mayo Clinic with us and was such a huge help to our spirits. During the day she would help take Philip to therapy, while I stayed with him at night.

So many family members and friends stepped up to the plate to help us so that our focus could be on Philip's rehabilitation. For my sister-in-law to be at the Mayo Clinic, her husband missed work to kept their three kids. My parents moved into our home to take care of our son. My in-laws kept Matthew during the day so that my parents could go to work. My mother-in-law stayed at my husband's office to keep things moving. She answered the phones and helped his assistant not be overwhelmed with running our businesses. Our CPA handled the books and paying bills. Our attorney drafted documents necessary for my mother-in-law to sign checks. Our banker processed the paperwork. Others kept me encouraged by sending e-mails and gifts and calling me on the phone.

Therapy sessions were divided into mornings and afternoons, separated by one hour for lunch. Philip told me how encouraging it was to come back to his room filled with flowers, cards, letters, and gifts, all waiting for him—such a bright spot in his day. He told me how empowering it was to know there were so many people praying and thinking about him and us. Even people whom he did not know reached out to help and pray!

We were told not to worry about anything other than getting Philip's health and mobility back. I struggled with the unknown future. I like to plan every detail of our lives and anticipate the next event. I realized "why" was not important. This question took too much energy away from focusing on the Lord and helping to restore Philip's health. Focusing on what was next took too much energy.

If you have ever had anyone you loved have a stroke, it feels like a death. People who have strokes talk about how it strips you of everything. I praise God for "team Wilson" while still having that feeling of walking blind into the unknown. God is in charge, but where are we going? I think about the difficult times in my life God pulled me through. He is the great "I am." He is sovereign and faithful. We just tried to press on in the unknown, waiting for God to change things as He had done many times in our lives before.

Remember God's Past Faithfulness

Philip Wilson

Oftentimes God demonstrates His faithfulness in adversity by providing for us what we need to survive. He does not change our painful circumstances. He sustains us through them. Charles Stanley

IT IS IMPORTANT NOT TO stand still during a storm, to keep moving forward. This is where our peace comes from, taking action. Moving forward is how God changes us and our circumstances and brings us to abundant life.

It is also very difficult to do. How tough it is to move past the initial anger of "Why did this happen to me?" and "This is not fair." But if we cannot figure out how to keep moving forward, we will get stuck and often miss God. I find it helpful to remember God's past faithfulness in my life. Remembering how God has brought me through past storms helps when facing the present storm. It creates a sense of anticipation of what God is going to do. Remembering past faithfulness helps our confidence and increases faith in God because of what He has done in the past.

The Israelites are a textbook case study of how God's plans can be short-circuited by our behavior. For years they cried out to God to be freed from the hands of the Egyptians. God answered, sending Moses and a series of very dramatic miracles. There could not have been much doubt in the Israelites' minds that God had an important role in their lives.

In Exodus 40:38, we read about how God even gave the Israelites a cloud to direct their path: "So the cloud of the Lord was over the tabernacle by day, and fire was in the cloud by night, in the sight of all the Israelites during all their travels." Still, the miracles did not seem to make much of a difference to the Israelites. Whenever times were tough, such as when there was a lack of food or water, they did not trust God for provisions; they grumbled. They forgot about what God had done. Their answer to tough times was to go back to Egypt and be slaves again. God kept them in the desert. Their trip to the Promised Land took forty years when it should have taken only two weeks.

If they had just obeyed God and stopped grumbling, they would have moved forward to the Promised Land. Whenever things got tough, they complained that God had left them. How could they have thought that way? After all the miracles, they still could not trust God to lead. I certainly wish I had a cloud of the Lord to show me the right direction to go.

Numbers 14:1–3 tell us about their troubles: "That night all the people raised their voices and wept aloud. All the Israelites grumbled against Moses and Aaron, and the whole assembly said to them "if only we had died in Egypt or in the desert. Why is the Lord bringing us to this land only to let us fall by the sword? Our wives and children will be taken as plunder. Would it not be better to for us to go back to Egypt?'"

Contrast the Israelites with Joseph. When Joseph was sold into slavery, he could have assumed God no longer controlled his destiny. When he was cast in jail for following God's laws of not committing adultery, he could have been angry at God. Some reward for being faithful!

There is a valuable lesson here. If we are to allow God to work through our trials, we must avoid grumbling, complaining, and blaming God for our troubles. We must move past asking why and move toward God, while waiting on Him to change things.

Remembering God's past faithfulness helps avoid grumbling. If you want God to work more through your trials, thank Him for what He has already done for you. Count your blessings. Focus on how He led you through past trials. Anticipate how God will lead you again. Celebrate how God will use the circumstance to bring glory to Him and change you in the process.

The Israelites could have thanked God for delivering them from slavery. Even though everything was not perfect, God was still at work. Yet they felt abandoned. They just wanted to go back to Egypt.

Celebrate past victories. God does not get you out of troubles but does promise to strengthen you to go through them. Do you remember times like this in your life? At the time we are at our weakest, feeling defeated, we must discipline ourselves to thank God for what he has already done in our lives and will do again.

Offer prayers like:

> "God, You have guided and sustained me through tough times before, and I expect You to do it again. Show me Your glory. I know You are at work. I cannot wait to see how. Allow my tough times to bring more glory to You. Use these tough times to mold me as You wish."

The mindset is that the battle is not yours but God's. You have reason to feel sorry for yourself, but no right to, because God is ready to help you through. Remembering how God was faithful in the past will help you move past the why, but you also need to trust that God is working now, even though you may not be able to see Him.

When we count our blessings and remember the ways God led us through past trials, our current problems have less of a presence in our lives. We don't care so much anymore about the why, and we can move forward a little easier. God was faithful before and He will be again. "Why" is not really important. We cannot wait to watch Him work.

Remember, faith is hope backed by a promise. We find strength and an increase in faith by remembering the past victories. Even though everything that happens to us may not seem to be good, when we trust God, He will work it out for good (this is His promise).

Remind yourself, while things happen that bring you harm, God will use them for our good. The more you are strengthened, the greater your faith, the greater the opportunity for God to turn your situation into something good. The battle belongs to God. You are His warrior. You have absolute confidence that He will see you through. He has before and will again. Figuring out why is just wasting your energy.

Remember, this is not your first storm and it won't be your last. Remember God's past faithfulness.

Today is Tuesday

Rhonda Wilson

Through humor, you can soften some of the worst blows that life delivers. And once you find laughter, no matter how painful your situation might be, you can survive it.
Bill Cosby

MY SISTER-IN-LAW AND PHILIP WERE hilarious together. The back-and-forth jabbing was very entertaining. They laughed so much and were so loud at times that the nurses came to our room to see what was going on. One nurse commented, "It sounds like you all are having a party in here. Keep it down."

One day my sister-in-law was thrown out of speech therapy and was told not to return. It seems she and Philip laughed at each other so much the therapist thought she needed to leave.

I asked Philip, "What happened? What were you laughing about?"

He said, "I was reading out loud but could not get through the material the therapist wanted me to read, because I would look at my sister and lose it."

I asked, "What were you reading?" He responded, "I was reading some statements that require a lot of tongue and air action. Statements like, 'Today is Tuesday,' and 'I want to buy some gasoline.'"

Even to this day I will be at a family gathering where one of them will say, "Today is Tuesday," and they both will burst out laughing. My sister-in-law was our comic relief and really helped me get through some tough days.

One day while we were on the rehab floor, I saw an informational video on stroke victims and their caregivers. I cried the entire time, realizing this could be our future. Things seemed hopeless. My day grew worse when at physical therapy Philip asked the therapist if he would ever run again. I knew he was thinking about the Mercedes Marathon. He had been training to run his first marathon, and the race was coming up in a few months. The therapist was not very encouraging. She thought it would take him a long time just to walk again and did not think he would ever be able to run again. His spirit was crushed.

That night I received a call from my parents about our son. It seems he began turning down all the family pictures, so he could not see our faces, and started referring to my parents as his mom and dad. My heart broke for the three-year-old.

The next day a test was done to see if Philip had a dissection of his brain artery. This is a condition that causes the arteries to separate from each other. The separation causes the vessel(s) to clot. The doctors had first seen this condition on Philip's MRI. This was not good news. It meant brain surgery, but they told me it was in an inoperable area. Nothing they could do. Again, we felt hopeless as the doctors plan to do another MRI the next day.

I called our pastor. At prayer meeting he led a church-wide prayer, calling for God's healing hand upon Philip. The next day we did the MRI. That night, around midnight, a surgeon, we had never met woke us. He stated that the neurologist had called him in to consult with us to offer advice on the possibility of brain surgery. We were both in a deep sleep and were trying to wake up and focus on what he was saying.

He said, "I cannot find the dissection anymore. It is gone."

He left the room and we sat in silence until Philip asked, "Was that an angel?" I said, "It is God, a miracle." We never saw the doctor again.

At the beginning of the second week, I could see Philip was ready to go home. He constantly asked the doctors "when." I could tell he was not going to stop asking until he got the answer he wanted.

The doctors wanted him to be at least independent before going home. Therapy would continue long after he went home, but they wanted to see if he could get around safely before releasing us. I loved seeing his determination! Once he knew what they wanted, he worked even harder on his therapy to make it happen. He was determined to go home by the end of the week. He said, "I am going home whether they let me or not. I want to see my son."

Every day, hour after hour, he improved. The first goal was to stand up from the wheelchair. Next he needed to stand by himself with help, and then without. Then he learned to take a few steps assisted, and then unassisted. Philip also wanted the therapist to teach him how to get down on the floor and get up, so he could play with Matthew. This took a lot of hard work because he did not have use of his left arm and only partial use of his right.

Before he went home he had to pass his final test:
- Walk outside around the hospital grounds.
- Get in and out of a car.
- Get around in a wheelchair.

He also had to meet with a psychiatrist to assess his mental state. They wanted him to take antidepressants, but he said that he was not depressed. I do not think they believed him. He told me after the meeting they asked him questions that seemed to assess his will to live.

Then came the news: you can go home. When packing to leave, the therapists asked him if he would like to take home the pottery sculptures he'd made during the week. He'd had recreation therapy that involved arts and crafts that would help with his limited dexterity and help him regain the ability to write.

He replied, "No thanks. I don't like turtles and never want to make another thing out of clay. I will never forgive my sister for signing me up for recreational therapy."

On the plane ride home, Philip was quiet and seemed to be holding back tears. He said to me, "I did not think we would ever see this day come." My mind went to thinking about how much we had suffered. I wondered what God's plan was in all this.

When we arrived at our home, we were met by the joys of our son. He ran into my arms and could not stop kissing and hugging Philip and me.

Matthew said, *"I did not think I would ever see you again, Daddy."*

Pressing Forward without Understanding

Philip Wilson

Life is like riding a bicycle. To keep your balance you must keep moving forward.
Albert Einstein

TO DISCOVER GOD'S PLAN FOR you while going through a storm, you must keep moving forward to not miss God. In addition to remembering God's past faithfulness, it is also helpful to press on by remembering how God changes us during our storms.

The Bible teaches that God is the same yesterday, today, and tomorrow. If God does not change, we must be the ones who change. The Bible promises abundant life in Christ and tribulation in this world. But which is it? Can the two exist at the same time?

James 1:2 says, "Count it all joy, my brothers, when you meet trials of various kinds." I do not consider suffering and going through trials a privilege; yet, living through adversity seems to bring positive change.

When we face trials, we are drawn closer to God. How we act when facing trials speaks volumes about what is going on inside us. Our suffering is part of how God matures us. We just do not develop in the same way without trials as we do with trials.

God often speaks to us in our hard times. During trials we seem to listen better. We are more humble and less busy. We are less likely to allow the noise of life to drown out God's still, small voice.

How involved God is in our lives or how much He loves us is not a reflection of our circumstances. When in the storms, do we respond, "Where is God in all this?" or do we accept the brokenness of the trial and embrace the changing of our hearts?

It is as if we think God does not know what is happening to us. Of course God knows what is going on with you. He knows your pain. He knows everything that is ever going to happen to you. He is God! How you handle your trials is either going to push you away from God or move you to Him.

One verse helps to underscore this. We read in 1 Peter 5:10, "And after you have suffered a little while, the God of all grace, who has called you to eternal glory in Christ, will himself restore, confirm, strengthen, and establish you."

This verse gives us a sense of a real, life-changing process that God puts us through to go from brokenness to glory. The key is what happens in us when storms happen to us.

The life of Joseph is a good example of how pain and suffering lead to glory for God. When adversity comes to us, it can be turned into something else. Joseph was sold into slavery but eventually became a powerful leader and saved his family from starvation. I would think anyone who has gone through what he went through would be bitter. I would think in his life there were times he cried out to God in confusion and pain, "Lord, are you even involved in my life?" He did not deserve what happened to him. But God took that pain and turned it into gain.

God used those events to mold Joseph into a leader and used him to impact others for God. What seemed unfair and not for his good was turned into something positive. The end result was glory to God.

As Christians we talk about conforming to the likeness of Christ. Conforming to the likeness of Christ means to shape our minds to think like Christ, to think eternally and focus on things above. The more we interpret the events in our life with an eternal meaning, the more we think like Christ. Adversity helps us to think like Christ by drawing us closer to Him. The closer we are, the more we think, act, and feel like Christ. It is the process of suffering that turns trials into glory for God and changes us for the better. Our lives are better equipped to help others through their storm. This is abundant life!

When we set our minds on things above, we love God for who He is, not what He can do for us. We praise God in all situations, regardless of the outcomes. We give first priority to carrying out God's will. Did Joseph lose faith in God? Did he remain faithful even though it seemed God was absent from his life? Absolutely!

An abundant life means to think eternally. Thinking eternally means to live pressing forward in faith. Even though we may not understand what is happening to us or why, we press on with an eternal focus. God may tell you why something happened or he may not. We will remain faithful, press on, and wait for God's direction.

When God does not seem to be doing anything, we keep on praying, keep on doing, and keep on staying in faith. Not an easy thing to do when in the midst of a storm.

One of Joel Osteen's sermons contains this good advice: "Don't put a question mark where God put a period." In other words, to move forward and read the next chapter in our lives means we have to stop asking why. God is moved by faith. Moving forward is an act of faith.

David was a great example of this. He had a sick baby. For a week he prayed over the baby. Everyone around him was concerned about his welfare. The baby died and David went to temple to worship. People around him were amazed and could not believe how he responded. He said that when the baby was alive, he prayed for God's healing; now that the child was gone, he could not bring him back but would one day be with him (2 Samuel 12:15–22).

In the same sermon, Osteen talks about how a car has a large windshield and a small rearview mirror. When you go through things you don't understand, you cannot move forward until you stop looking behind to the past. You must forget what is behind and press on in faith, because God is always writing the next chapter of your life.

A great illustration of how God relates to us is found in Scripture when God compares us to eagles. When baby eagles are young, their mother pushes them out of the nest so they can learn to fly. I imagine the baby eagle thinking, *Mom*

36

have you lost your mind? This is not good for me. Yet this is the process by which a baby learns how to fly. We must have faith that God's plan is for our benefit even though often we don't see it.

The storms in life can change us for the better or for the worse. We may not like the process or even enjoy it, but we cannot argue with the results. What we need is better acceptance of the process. We need to change how we view suffering. ✗

Think about how our kids motivate us to do things. Do you enjoy sitting at the baseball field all day, being cooked by the sun? Do you enjoy playing dress-up and having a tea party or changing poopy diapers? We do these things because we love our kids. With our kids, it is all about them. We put aside our wants and desires and put their needs at the forefront.

Contrast this with your love for God. Do you feel the same way about enduring your trials and bringing glory to God? Is it a joy, as Scripture says? I don't think you have to enjoy your trial, but is your love for God more important than your will? Do you accept the suffering because it brings glory to God?

Tough times experienced in life, unfortunately sometimes do not lead to an abundant life nor bring glory to God, even though God promises He can use every situation, good or bad, to his glory. Sometimes this is just not the case. Either His promise is not true or we are doing something to prevent Him from working through our storms.

Romans 8:28 tells us, "We are assured and know that all things work together and are for good to those who love God and are called according to his purpose."

Not just some, but all things. When faced with tough times, what can we do so our trials are not wasted? God did not give us a choice: trials will happen. So why are so many people wiped out by the storms while others experience spiritual leaps forward? What did the person who grew through a tough time do that those who are wiped out did not?

I think the answer goes back to the discussion of moving past "why." When bad things happen, our first response is to ask why, out of anger. There just seems to be something in our DNA that wants to know why things are happening to us, and especially we want to know what to expect in the future.

Adam and Eve are examples of this. Their desire to eat from the tree of knowledge of good and evil is a lesson about human nature. Before we live and press forward, we like answers. We want knowledge of why, and we want to know the future. Living without being prepared for what is to come makes us uncomfortable. We like to know cause and effect: this thing happened because of that thing.

The key is to endure our trials and to press forward without understanding why something is happening, or where we are going. God does not mind when we ask why, or even if we get angry when trials happen to us. Yet for God to do anything in our lives, there are times when we must move forward without understanding.

I see people all the time who are stuck. They are confused and discouraged by their situation and cannot see how God could be at work. They cannot move to a point of asking God to lead their next step. This is a decision we must make to be faithful and to continue on, while waiting on God. If we are going to allow God's work in our lives, we must figure out how to keep on praying, keep on believing, keep on obeying, and keep on doing what we know is right.

When people are suffering, they often hear "rely on His strength" from other Christians. What does that mean? Does it mean that when we are faced with tough times, we step aside and do nothing, that we just say, "Here, God, work it out"? The Christian life is a partnership process with God. We do our part; He does His. God is not going to do something for us that we can do for ourselves. Sometimes it is difficult to know when our responsibility stops and starts, but we have responsibility. We cannot just sit back and let God do everything. Our involvement is crucial.

We must figure out how to not get stuck. We must focus externally on things above and not our current situation. We need discipline to move forward, focusing on who God is, and not what He could do for us. We must press on in faith, not knowing where we are going or why something is happening. We remain in faith, believing whatever comes our way, God will eventually work it out for good.

So is God good all the time? *Maybe our definition of good is not the same as God's.* What does a child say is good? Often what I've seen is that a "good" situation is when children get whatever they want, when they want it. In this attitude, children want to be in charge. We know that is not the best thing for them and we know what will happen if they are in charge, but their minds cannot grasp how selfish this is. Children complain about everything and have a difficult time appreciating anything they have.

When we go through trials, we are tested. God expects our trust. The Lord loves those He chastises. He breaks us so He can use us. Forget the need to understand why. Forget the need to see the future.

Knowing why does not help us move forward. It is an act of faith, a choice only each person can make. We have to learn to make the choice.

Date Night

Rhonda Wilson

The difference between stumbling blocks and stepping stones is how you use them.
Unknown

IT HAS BEEN A YEAR since our times at the Mayo Clinic. Over the past year we have experienced the birth of our daughter, Matthew's entering four-year-old preschool, and many days of therapy for Philip. My days were spent with diaper changes, feedings, snuggles, playing with the kiddos, and encouraging Philip.

Our focus was on God's leading and His will for our lives. We consciously tried to keep our focus on the here and now, not the uncertainties of the future. It was hard. We still had so many questions; those unknowns still lingered: Will Philip be able to go back to work? Will I need to go back to work? If I do, who will take care of the kids? How long will our savings last? Are we going to lose our house?

In the midst of all these disconcerting thoughts, Philip and I planned a date night. We had not had an opportunity to get away. As we talked over dinner, our conversation was on the many storms and bright spots of the year. I looked across the table at my best friend and whispered a "thank you" to God, for Philip's life and for His perfect will for our family.

But then reality struck! Everything was not ok. There were still so many things Philip could not do, especially things I cherished, like:
- opening doors for me
- walking hand-in-hand
- spending time together running errands, and going to sporting events and church
- exercising together

Philip, as the result of the stroke, had very little balance. He needed his arms free to walk. He still did not have use of his left arm, so it remained limp at his side. How grateful I was that he could walk, but I missed holding hands and doing the many activities we enjoyed together.

Loneliness reared its ugly head in those days after the stroke, as Philip slept more than twelve hours a day. With a new baby and our four-year-old son, Philip and I were not able to spend much time together. Because of physical limitations, he found it challenging to help around the home or take care of the kiddos. All "man-power" was spent on therapy and getting better.

Matthew was affected too, and one day he said sadly, "Daddy can't play ball with me or carry me anymore."

That night at dinner Philip talked about some of the difficulties he was facing with his limitations and what it would mean for our future: "It is not easy to wash your hair with one arm. It is even harder to tie your shoes. I have got to get back to work; we need money." I loved his feistiness. He would not stand around and let others do things for him. It might take an hour to get ready in the morning, but he wanted to do it for himself. He did ask me for help from time to time, but I had to learn very quickly to let him try. My nature is to help without him asking, but I knew it was important to him and his self-image as a man to do as much for him-self as possible.

His positive attitude and grateful heart about life came through when he would talk about the unexpected blessings. He talked about how special it was to be around the house for the first year of Caroline's life—how many fathers can say they spent every day with their baby during the first year of their life?—and how he enjoyed spending more time with Matthew and riding along with me to pick him up from "Mother's Day Out." He apologized for being around the home all the time but not helping much: "I am a housewife, or at least one that does not do any work."

41

He also wrote his first book, about money, while healing from the stroke. Amazing, if you ask me! There was no sitting around and moping for him! He pecked away at the computer for months, thinking and writing. The intellectual time spent on the book sharpened his mind. He talked about the book being a legacy for him if he had another stroke and died. He wanted to know that someday his kids could read about what Daddy did, and how he helped people with their finances. He joked: "This book is a lot more work than I thought it would be. Oh well, so what? I need something to do. There's only so much Judge Judy a man can watch."

He also spoke about the frequent feeling of death. It did not seem he feared it, but his body would feel strange, with twinges of pain at times, alarming him and me. "Am I having another stroke?" he would ask. He told me at times he would fear drifting off to sleep, not knowing if he would awaken. It was very difficult for him to live with the fear of having another stroke. He thought that if he did, it would surely kill him. He didn't feel as though he could be that lucky again, to make it through another stroke.

I focused on the things my husband could do and my love and commitment to him. It wasn't always easy, but with the Lord's help and prayers from so many, my mind stayed on God and the needs of our family . . . hoping Philip would get stronger and better soon.

It seemed Philip was struggling mentally, as I was. I asked if he was having spiritual warfare. He mentioned that he worried night and day about our financial future. I was not surprised to find out about his struggle. He has always taken very seriously the responsibility of providing for his family.

My War Within

Rhonda Wilson

For our struggle is not against flesh and blood, but against the rulers, against the powers, against the world forces of this darkness, against the spiritual forces of wickedness in the heavenly places. Ephesians 6:13

OVER THE PAST FEW YEARS some battles have been going on within my mind. I think about the war within. The storms of life take a toll not only on our physical being but also our minds. There is a raging war that only God can claim the victory in. And it is through Him we can fight our battles.

I have found to fight the war within there are several important truths to remember, including:

- See ourselves as God sees us; no stinky thinking allowed.
- Set our minds on things above.
- Refuse to function in a destructive spirit.
- Know that the battle is won before it begins.
- A prayer life is a powerful life.

To fight this war within, we need to remember how God sees us and avoid stinky thinking. At the Mayo Clinic after Philip's stroke, my mind kept racing with thoughts of the worst-case scenario. I wondered whether Philip would ever be somewhat normal again and run that marathon race he had so earnestly been seeking to do. These thoughts turned my focus toward anger and bitterness. It was at this time I learned from experience that we cannot function while "stinky thinking." Nor do we want this stinky thinking to affect those around us. It's a contagious mind-set that will soon spiral into despair. Our words either help or hurt us. That is why the Bible tells us to focus and keep our minds on the Lord. We must see ourselves as God sees us. Isaiah 26:3 says, "You will keep in perfect peace Him whose mind is steadfast, because He trusts in you."

43

During those difficult days I felt God saying to me, "Remember my promises and truths." The Bible tells us we do not wage war with this world or the things of this world, but this war is with the Evil One, who is out to devour and destroy us. In 1 Peter 5:8 we read, "Your enemy the devil prowls around like a roaring lion looking for someone to devour."

The Bible talks about setting our thoughts on things above. It implies action. This is spiritual warfare, when two opposing attitudes or "spirits" collide with each other. It is our choice, His way or the Enemy's way. Bottom line, which will you choose? It is a conscious choice to continually stay focused on Him by reading and studying His Word, daily.

It's crucial for us to focus our lives around Him and His Word, rather than fitting God around our lives of busyness. This was a vital activity for me—to maintain my time with Him to maintain a positive direction and keep His priorities in order. It would have been so easy for me to be distracted by all the things I had to do just to afunction on a day-to-day basis.

To fight the war within we need to refuse to function in the destructive spirit. When facing a storm in life, we are tempted to be bitter and negative about our situation. We short-circuit God's work in our lives to work it out for our good. The best antidote to the destructive spirit that I have found is thankfulness. We defeat the Enemy by operating in the spirit of thankfulness. Thank God for every little and big event in your life.

I'm reminded of the events around Philip's strokes and how even he thanked the caretakers for their help and service to him. We thanked God for the doctors, nurses, friends, and family who so patiently served and helped in the care of him. That thankfulness was a tremendous help with his mindset and helped him (and me) avoid a destructive spirit. In thanking God for everything, our minds are focused on Him, rather than on our problems. He will take care of the problem as we continually keep pressing on and focusing on Him.

44

Another way to fight the war within is by remembering that the war has already been won. To do this we need to defuse the enemy's attacks by continually functioning out of God's kingdom of love, joy, peace, kindness, justice, grace, trust, mercy, wholeness, and compassion, rather than the Evil One's kingdom of evil, hatred, discouragement, deceit, anger, condemnation, suspicion, accusation, and shame. We know God provides spiritual armor to fight this war and has already claimed the victory before the battle begins. Ephesians 6:10 exhorts: "Finally, be strong in the Lord and His mighty power. Put on the full armor of God so that you can take your stand against the devil's schemes." And then in verses 13–18, Paul describes the armor that strengthens us during difficult times:

Put on the full armor of God, so that when the day of evil comes, you may be able to stand your ground, and after you have done everything, to stand. Stand firm then with the belt of truth [His truth] buckled around your waist, with the breastplate of righteousness [right living] in place, and with your feet fitted with the readiness that comes from the gospel of peace.

In addition to all this, take up the shield of faith, with which you can extinguish all the flaming arrows of the evil one. Take the helmet of salvation and the sword of the Spirit, which is the Word of God. And pray in the Spirit on all occasions with all kinds of prayers and requests. With this in mind, be alert and always keep on praying for all the saints.

Standing in the midst of the storm, our battle has already been won. God will claim the victory! He already has.

And finally, the most important weapon for the war within is the power of prayer. Prayer is a privilege and a powerful weapon against the Evil One and his schemes. We defeat the arrows of doubt and defeat through prayer by focusing on God. A prayerful life is a powerful life!

As a practical matter, I know it can be a challenge to concentrate on prayer. I like to read a verse, study it, and then pray. I find this to be an effective way to turn our eyes on Him.

45

My War Within

Philip Wilson

If God were not my friend, Satan would not be so much my enemy.
Thomas Brooks

WHEN PRESSING FORWARD, AN ONGOING issue is the mental spiritual warfare. Listening to the voice in your head makes it tough to trust God: What are you going to do?

So what are you going to do? Sometimes friends and family can feed the monster without meaning to, by asking the same question. This was an area of significant struggle for me after my stroke.

Before the stroke we were doing pretty well, or at least we were by the world's standards. I had been building my own business for twenty years, and things were going well. We lived in a nice home in a good neighborhood, drove new cars, and even had vacation homes at the beach and at the lake. Most people looking from the outside in would say we had it pretty good.

During the first twelve months after the stroke, we needed to sell the majority of our assets just to pay bills. My income was 150 percent less than the previous year's income. In other words, even though I was not working and still recovering, the expenses of the business continued.

The second year after the stroke, I went back to work part-time and was able to make enough money to cover the business overhead, but still I had very little personal income. Tithing and offerings were a bit of a challenge during those days and came from savings or were borrowed from lines of credit.

It was not until the third year that I actually had a positive income, though it was still more than a 95 percent reduction from the years before the stroke. Two years with no income and then a 95 percent pay cut.

Around that time, 2008, the economy started heading off the cliff. The financial world was hit hard. The stock market plunged. Even at my best, without physical issues to contend with, it would have been tough to maintain our pre-stroke financial lives. The country was struggling. The financial services world was dying a quick death. It was not a great time to be connected to the financial industry or to have your primary assets in real estate and stocks.

We continued to sell our assets. Before the stroke, I once thought we were doing pretty well with some real estate and stock market investments, only to see those assets deteriorate to the point of little or no equity or value. We cashed in my retirement and used our kids' college funds. In some cases when real estate assets were sold, we were upside down and had to borrow money to clear the mortgage. The sales price was not sufficient to cover the debt, but I could not make the payment to keep the asset, and we needed to get rid of it or eventually go into default and lose the asset to the bank.

I sold the commercial building I'd spent five years designing, locating, and building. When I built it I thought I would spend every day of my working life there, and now we needed to sell it. To make matters worse, we sold at a huge loss. We were happy to get anything out of it. We gave an offering from the proceeds to the church to be used for a game room in the gym.

We had seen a video one Sunday about how the church provided an afterschool hangout to keep kids out of trouble. We both realized the need for it, with working parents in our community.

We sold most of our rental properties and even my "dream" lake house. I had wanted a lake house since high school and never believed it would happen. We sold it at a huge loss, as well as our boat, watercraft, and all the lake toys. In all, we lost several million dollars of net worth and incurred additional debt that we will be paying back for the rest of our lives. I learned what it feels like to wake up feeling good about things and go to bed with your world totally turned upside down. I remembered being taught as a kid that if you have to have something to be happy, then you don't need it, because our security comes from the Lord.

47

Nevertheless, I did not feel very secure.

We tithed on the sale of all our assets, even though at times we had to borrow to make the tithe. I know that may seem strange, but we just felt like we should. We did not have regret about having to sell, but we did wonder about the future security of our family. Most of what I have worked for the past twenty years had vanished. How I worried night and day about our future. The worry was always with me. I just could not shake it.

The Sin of Worry

Philip Wilson

Worry does not empty tomorrow of its sorrow, it empties today of its strength.
Corrie ten Boom

ANXIETY IS TRYING TO FIGURE out tomorrow, today. When going through a storm, are you frozen by worry? Does your need to know the future prevent God's working in your life that day? The Bible is very specific on this subject. "But seek first his kingdom and his righteousness, and all these things will be given to you as well. Therefore do not worry about tomorrow, for tomorrow will worry about itself. Each day has enough trouble of its own" (Matthew 6:33–34).

Worry is spiritual warfare. Complaining about your situation is sin. No matter how hard you think you have it, someone has it worse. The Bible says God is working in your life at every minute, in ways you do not see or understand. He is always present with us. God is with us when we get up, when we go to bed, and every minute in between. God is trying to teach us to trust Him to direct our steps.

He is the great "I am." He is here; He is present. *God's will is done through us, not apart from us.* He is actively at work in our lives, to fulfill His will. When we face problems, God will either take them away or He won't. If God does not take problems away, we must trust God to see us through and know He has a plan. I know, we would much rather He take our problems away.

There is nothing that comes against us that God cannot work out for our good. Trying to figure out the next move is a waste of time and energy. God is in charge. We must have real faith in God. *Real faith is bringing you to the point of not knowing the future. Worry sees the problem, but faith sees the God who will walk you through it.*

In 1 Corinthians 10:13, we read: "No temptation has overtaken you except what is common to mankind. And God is faithful; he will not let you be tempted beyond what you can bear. But when you are tempted, he will also provide a way out so that you can endure it."

The Bible talks about being "more than a conqueror," meaning you are certain of the victory before you even have a problem. We just need to learn how to be patient. Some things in life are inevitable, like waiting, disappointment, and failure. We just do not like to be patient. It is okay to think about problems and even consider actions we can take, but at some point we realize there are things we have no control over.

Turning to 2 Corinthians 12:8, we read: "Three times I pleaded with the Lord about this, that it should leave me. But he said to me, 'My grace is sufficient for you, for my power is made perfect in weakness.' Therefore I will boast all the more gladly of my weaknesses, so that the power of Christ may rest upon me."

What is meant by power made perfect in weakness? God's grace is the power of the Holy Spirit that comes to you, enabling you to do with ease what you never could do on your own.

God wants us to live life one day at a time and be dependent on Him for the day, not tomorrow. Grace is also given to us for the day: what we need today, not tomorrow. Look at the Israelites. God gave them provision every day, but only what they could gather for that day. They had to trust God for tomorrow. In other words, no worrying!

God is the great "I am," not "I was" or "I will be." *Life is not meant to be lived in the past or future, but today.* Learn to take the attitude "it is what it is." There are some things you cannot change. Worry may make you feel better, but it ignores God's command to trust Him. It is a sin! Joyce Meyer describes worry as sitting in a rocking chair and rocking all day. It keeps you busy but you never get anywhere.

50

Worry does not manipulate God into action. Sometimes we think it does. Stop dwelling on what is wrong with your life. Don't magnify your problems with worry; magnify God. Start the day with "I am a child of God, I am created to bring Him glory." Start your day with words of praise, and not words of worry.

Start your day being thankful, and say so to God. We complain because we feel we deserve better than our current circumstances. We don't deserve anything. Celebrate your journey; the best is yet to come.

We move in the direction of our thoughts. Whatever you focus on grows in your mind. If you rise every morning focusing on the negative, you are probably going to have a negative day. I am not saying you need to trick yourself into thinking everything is fantastic. This is not prosperity gospel mumbo jumbo.

When you get up in the morning, praise God for who He is, what He has done, and what He will do. Live life amazed. Begin the day with a sense of anticipation of what God will do that day. What are you worried about? The creator of the universe is in control. He created you and has given you a plan and a purpose for your life. You have the power of God inside of you. How can you worry?

Sometimes our worry comes from concerns about consequences of our making. If you have made a mistake and worry about consequences, give it to God. Ask God to allow your mistakes to bring Him glory. Repent and move forward.

King David ordered a man to be killed so he could take his wife. He repented but still had to pay a heavy price. Yet he still moved forward. His life was in God's hands; he pressed on and did not worry about what would happen next. God was in control of his life.

David had another son after the first one died. The Bible says the son became the wisest person in the world. His name was Solomon. I would think his father had a big role in how wise Solomon became. David used his mistakes to bring glory to God through his son. He could have sat around in self-pity, worrying about the future, regretting the past, but he kept moving forward, trusting God.

When we become absorbed in worry, we miss God. Our worries cause us to miss God's amazing work. We are so engrossed in our own lives. Because of this, we don't see God working, and then we complain He is not around or involved. Self-involvement has caused us to be almost totally numb to His presence. Do what you can do, and leave what you can't do to God. Stop worrying about things you cannot control. Cast your cares on the great change agent, and sit back and watch Him at work.

Seven Years After the Stroke

Rhonda Wilson

Life is 10 percent what happens to me and 90 percent how I react to it.
Charles Swindoll

PHILIP AND I SPENT a Friday together, going to breakfast, drinking coffee, and running errands. We so enjoyed our time together and were grateful to God for our friendship and marriage. Our lives again took shape as Philip's business was improving. He was happy and physically feeling good. I, on a similar note, had grown in my own managing of the "worry area," giving most of my worries to God and no longer listening to the Evil One's lies. Matthew had begun fourth grade, and Caroline began kindergarten. Life was rocking along.

An interesting story Philip told me at breakfast was about a time when Matthew was five years old. Philip had taken him to the local fire station to see the fire trucks. Matthew so enjoyed trucks and cars, and how they worked. The normally busy fire station was quiet, with the shiny fire trucks lined up all in a row. Matthew was so excited! As Matthew and Philip were talking to the firemen, one kept scrunching up his eyes and tilting his head to the side as he stared at Philip.

"Do I know you?" the fireman asked.

Philip smiled and said, "I don't think so."

The fireman asked, "Have I ever been to your house on a call?"

My husband mentioned to him that he'd had a stroke in 2005, and the fireman replied, "That's it!"

Philip said, "How do you remember that so many years later? You must have had hundreds of calls to homes since then." The fireman responded, "That is true, but we don't get calls to help thirty-nine-year-olds who've had a brainstem stroke and then see them walking around later. That type of stroke is the worst kind you can have. A lot of brain activity is handled by the brainstem. Most people die."

It still takes my breath away when I think about this. We knew Philip's recovery was a miracle and were grateful to God for His work in Philip's life and in our family. Things were going well, with life progressing to some sort of "normal," though normal for us was called "a new normal." But just as we were getting comfortable and in our routines, April 23, 2012, rang in with a loud boom.

At my son's soccer game, the laughter and squeals from our children brought a smile to my face. Then boom! My smile immediately faded to panic and confusion. Upon arriving at the scene of an explosion, I saw a child lying on the ground with people around her. I didn't recognize her as our daughter, Caroline, until I saw the clothes she was wearing. I screamed in agony, "It's Caroline!" Our six-year-old daughter had been severely burned by a transformer that had exploded.

Matthew, her hero, was the one who ran for help. We were thankful for Matthew's persistence as someone listened to his cries of, "It's my sister!"

My dad reached Caroline, lifting her lifeless body, still on fire, away from the transformer, yelling for people to call 9-1-1. An ER doctor who just happened to be walking by heard the explosive sound and went into crisis mode, breathing life into her motionless body. An ER nurse just happened to be there and helped to find a weak pulse in Caroline's thigh, as no pulse was found earlier.

As I arrived on the scene, I was in shock but somehow was able to encourage sweet Caroline: "Fight! You can do it. Come on, baby, breathe. Breathe, baby, breathe! Oh dear God, please help her breathe!"

My skin and body tingled from seeing her lifeless, singed, and burned body lying before me, at first unrecognizable except for her clothes and her pink Keen shoes. My eyes fell on my husband; his head was on the ground, sobbing in agony. We looked at each other and were blown away by the scene: this was our Caroline. The whole thing was surreal.

A lifesaver helicopter arrived and Caroline was loaded onto it to go to the hospital. Besides hearing the blades of the spinning helicopter, I heard prayer warriors standing and praying all around. The prayers sounded so loud, yet mumbled, as if they were being spoken in my ears, but it's His ears that are fervently listening to the cries of His saints.

I know Philip drove my dad and me to Children's Hospital, but I still don't know how we got there. Philip was driving and sobbing as I sat next to him in shock, calling my prayer warriors to pray. It felt like we would see Caroline again.

At the hospital, we saw Caroline for the first time. She was smiling! Yes, she was actually smiling. Smiling through this storm already . . . love her heart!

We were told Caroline had been severely burned over 40 percent of her body and would be hospitalized for three to six months. Tests were being run to determine if all internal organs were functioning normally. We would not find out until later in the week, but at that point her heart and all vital organs were functioning. I whispered, "Thank you, God."

Caroline sustained third-degree burns all around her right arm and along her torso and bottom area, with second-degree burns on her face, back, and left leg. She was expected to need multiple skin graft surgeries.

Most people would never survive an electrical accident such as this, but Caroline had so far. Her spirit was strong. For now, the nurses subdued her with morphine to ease her pain.

To say I prayed constantly is an understatement! I think I breathed constant prayers the whole time. I thanked God for the angels He placed around Caroline at the exact time she needed them at the accident. God was there! I continue to thank Him for Matthew, who was diligent in his cries for help and smartly thought to not pick up Caroline and injure himself in the process. His smart and quick thinking saved her life! My heart wells with gratefulness of His hand in the people, nurses, doctors, and staff and all His blessings along this journey. God reached down to comfort us through His people.

At the scene, one of my sweet friends kept rubbing my back as I held our burned and charred daughter. That hand upon me was the hand of God bringing comfort to His distraught child. I remember the voices of people praying behind me that night. I was so thankful for them and their boldness in lifting us all up to Him.

Was It God's Will that Our Daughter was Electrocuted?

Philip Wilson

One of the marks of spiritual maturity is the quiet confidence that God is in control without the need to understand why He does what He does.

Anonymous

MOST PEOPLE GOING THROUGH a storm want an understanding of the will of God and how it affects their lives and how the decision of others affect God's will. We may ask, "How do we know God's will for us?" If a person gets drunk and kills someone while behind the wheel, is this the will of God? How does a person's sin affect God's plan?

If God is sovereign and chooses not to stop something from happening, then isn't it His will? If it is not God's will, then why did He not stop it? Is He not able to? How can a sovereign God not be able to stop something? That would not make much sense. If someone has cancer and it is the will of God, then fighting against the disease is opposing the will of God. If cancer is not the will of God, then why does He allow it? Was it God's will our daughter was electrocuted, or was it just the negligence of others? Or was it because she was in the wrong place at the wrong time?

A great way to understand the answers to these questions is to look at the death of Jesus. Was it the will of God to put Jesus to death? Or was it the sinful actions of Judas, Pilate, and many others that accomplished this? If it was not God's will that Jesus be put to death, then why did He not stop it? If He could not stop it, then does sin stop God? Does the evil of this world prevent God from working?

If humans have a choice, then our will must sometimes intersect with God's will, because our choices will not always be God's choice; otherwise we would never have a choice and God (and what God wants) would determine our choices. We would be robotic followers of God's, puppets on a string in God's play. If we are free to choose, our choices sometimes will be wrong and conflict with God's will. Then what happens?

57

When bad things happen to us, many people respond, "Well, everything happens for a reason." This is a bit of a cop-out. Not everything that happens to us is the will of God. Saying everything happens for a reason seems to help us accept our circumstances, but it is still a cop-out.

It was not the will of God for His Son to be put to death on a cross. See Acts 2:36: "Therefore let all Israel be assured of this: God has made this Jesus, whom you crucified, both Lord and Messiah."

The will of God was for this world to accept Him, repent of their sins, and follow. The Bible says before the world was formed God wanted salvation for us through Jesus. See 1 Peter 1:18–20: "For you know that it was not with perishable things such as silver or gold that you were redeemed from the empty way of life handed down to you from your ancestors, but with the precious blood of Christ, a lamb without blemish or defect. He was chosen before the creation of the world, but was revealed in these last times for your sake."

It was not God's will that Jesus die on a cross. This method of execution was man's choice. *God willed salvation.* Circumstance brought about by evil men caused Jesus to be put to death. In those circumstances the will of God for man's redemption was achieved. The higher goal of salvation was brought about through the evil (sin).

How Jesus came to be our Savior could have been brought about in a number of ways. It was the law of man at the time to put criminals to death through crucifixion. God allowed those circumstances to happen but did not allow them to defeat His ultimate purpose, which was salvation. Consider sickness. Many people feel sickness is God's will, but perfect health is the will of God. If sickness was the will of God, when you seek medical help to get well you would be fighting against the will of God. That does not make much sense. A body free of disease is more effective for God than one with disease.

58

But people get sick anyway, sometimes because of environment, and many times by our own actions. If you drink and smoke and overeat, you may die prematurely and probably will get sick along the way.

There is a will of God within sinful circumstances. We must choose God's will in our sickness as if we had never been sick. There is that possibility of sickness but also the possibility of our reaction to the sickness that brings so much glory to God that the sickness is justified. In other words, God gives us a choice. That choice may be the wrong one sometimes, but He gives us the freedom to choose. Our choices, even though wrong, are still used by God to fulfill His will. Through sickness we are often more in line with God's will for our lives than if we were healthy. God allows sickness, which moves us to Him and toward His will and brings glory to Him. Through the sickness God brings change. If this is true of sickness, it must be true of all our circumstances.

Replace the word "sickness" with "tough times." There is that possibility of tough times, but also the possibility of our reaction to the tough times that brings so much glory to God that the tough times are justified. So by allowing sickness and storms, which may have even been caused by our own sin or the sin of someone else, the end result is change in us and glory to God.

The Bible says Jesus has overcome the world, but Jesus is not the ruler of this world. The Devil is the ruler of this world. When we see the evil in the world, we need to see God's goodness. We cannot see good if we cannot recognize evil. If we did not see the evil, then how would we know if something was good? God uses man's sinful choices to fulfill his will. God intended for us to follow Jesus but used our rejection of his Son to bring about salvation anyway. Ultimately, His will, despite sin, will be done.

Was it God's will that Caroline, my daughter, be electrocuted? No, but even though it was because of others' negligence, God's glory will shine through. I have no doubt God is using Caroline to bring Him glory through the accident. I have no doubt God is changing her life and the lives of people around her through what happened to her. I have no doubt that God is changing our whole family through her accident.

So what could God be up to by allowing the accident? Often we have no idea. It still comes back to a trust of God being in control. Ultimately, His will for our lives will be done. We just need to sit back and let Him work.

THIS CHAPTER IS NOT REALLY A CHAPTER but a series of blog posts, written by Rhonda, during Caroline's hospital stay and the days after. This was not an easy time for us, but we recognized God's goodness and, yes, at times, funniness in the storms of life. We wanted to include the stories in the book to help the reader further understand our message. Throughout the blog you can see God's glory all over our situation. You can see the blessing and the change that took place in our lives and the lives of others.

First Hospital Days

Caroline got a feeding tube in her nose yesterday afternoon to help her get more nourishment in her little body. Her right arm is severely burned and is heavily bandaged, as well as bandages covering her whole body from head to toe. The great news is Caroline is still moving her fingers. Blood is still flowing there! The doctors have been concerned she might have circulation issues that could result in loss of her arm.

I was in her hospital room yesterday when she was wheeled back after her daily bath and bandage changes. When she saw me, she tried to smile and wiggled the fingers on her right hand to wave.

Her face is swollen and doesn't look like Caroline. But her feisty spirit is there and she is quick to smile even in these circumstances. Caroline has been kept pretty sedated, but yesterday she asked Philip for some sips of water and told me she was ready to go home. Her internal organs seem to be working well: no kidney damage, no heart damage, no brain damage. It is a miracle!! Caroline is now considered "stable, not critical." The nurses and doctors want her to get up and move around a bit in order to stretch her skin, but understandably she does not want to. It is uncomfortable for her.

I am so thankful for your e-mails, cards, food, gifts, visits, hugs, and most of all your prayers. It has so warmed our hearts! We continue to thank God for the miracles we are seeing and the loving angels He has placed in our life. He is so good.

A funny from Caroline . . . her sense of humor and making light of the situation is incredible! To handle the pain, Caroline and I were taught to sniff a flower and blow out the candles. While Mommy's sniffing and blowing, Caroline says, "Mommy, can you stop blowing, your breath smells!" I told her it was "morning breath." Then she breathed and asked if her breath smelled. I told her it smelled like roses!

Another story that touched our hearts, a dear friend of ours came to see Caroline and said, "Caroline, I'm sure you've been showing a bunch of Jesus to everyone here." She nodded yes and said, "Yeah, but I think I can show more . . ."

Caroline is still in pain and trying so hard to be the brave and strong girl that she is. She amazes us with her fight to get better. One day I caught a sweet conversation between Caroline and her daddy, Philip said, "I'm sorry you are going through this." She replied, "It's okay, Daddy."

Philip replied, "No, Caroline, it's not! This is not fair."

I do sometimes worry about Caroline's future. Will Caroline ever get married and have a loving husband who is blinded to her burn scars? Will she be made fun of? Will her arm be able to fully function? But God assures us He is always in control. I know He is with her and will strengthen her to share her story and His.

Getting Better

After a week in the hospital, the doctors say it is time for Caroline's first skin graft surgery. I hope and pray this will provide relief for her and encouragement toward recovery. She is a fighter and has shown such great courage in the midst of the storm. The doctor mentioned her right arm would be the challenge, since it was severely burned. But I am forever thankful she still has it!

I pray for God to be glorified through this. The Evil One has already lost the battle.. lives are changing due to Him being revealed. I am amazed by our friends and their diligent prayers and outpouring of love and support! How did we ever get to be so blessed by so many friendships?

Caroline's pain can be unbearable at times. She almost passed out today from the pain when her right arm was being put in a splint. I know this is to help her, but it's not easy seeing an innocent little girl in pain. I am comforted by remembering God knows and loves her even more deeply than we do. To Him, the glory now and forever!

I'm ecstatic. The doctor says if all goes well these next few days, Caroline will be able to go home! The doctor keeps saying she's a miracle! I know our God is the Great Physician and has a plan and a purpose for her life as well as ours.

Surgery

Caroline's skin graft surgeries have all gone well. Philip and I are able to see her body for the first time since her accident. She is beautiful! My heart is so grateful to God! Every essential area was missed by the electrical current. Skin grafts look amazingly well, like a screen window, but flesh color.

We learn how to massage Caroline, to blend the grafts in with her skin. This was so painful for her... my heart is praying the whole time she's screaming in pain. I know it will help her, but it's painful for me because I'm hurting the poor child. I love seeing Philip and Caroline's relationship rise to a new level of closeness. He's been so encouraging and good with her. They are so precious to watch!

I heard someone say today, "God loves us through other people." The avalanche of love, prayers, concern, offers of help, visits, and other acts of kindness upon Caroline and our family has made God's love visible and deeply felt. I see God's glory all around!

Girl's Night

It's girl's night here at Children's Hospital. We had a sword fight with toothbrushes (don't worry, we washed them), a pillow fight consisting of Caroline punching the pillow, a marathon reading of the Magic Fairy books. We even snuck out of her room for a midnight (9:30 p.m.) stroll down the hall of the burn unit.

Caroline beat her momma to the end of the hallway and giggled! I was afraid they'd throw us out! Everyone else was asleep! We did say little prayers for each child as we passed their rooms. Caroline wanted to draw pictures for them to "help them feel better."

I'm still amazed at God's hand in all this! I feel like we owe Him our life! He saved one of His precious children for us to continue to raise. My heart wells with such gratitude that I want to please Him even more and share His hope.

Caroline's Home

What an exciting day . . . Caroline came home! Three weeks (not six months) after her accident, Caroline comes home! Upon first arriving home her comment was, "Well, I guess we can take the pink bows down now. I'm home!"

Pink is her favorite color, and bows had been placed around the neighborhood. I told her, "Sweet one, they are still there as a reminder that you are loved and people will still be praying for you and your body to heal so you can do all the fun things children do."

Caroline said with a smile: "Oh, okay!"
Everyone is so excited to see Caroline! Matthew especially! He ran out to greet her with a smile and a "now can I touch her" look. Caroline leaned into him and he knew it was fine to hug. Such a sweet moment!

Caroline first took a tour of the house, to be sure all was as it was before, especially her bedroom. But one place in particular caught her eye... the dining room with all the love you could fit in there. Gifts upon gifts: cards, toys, music, blankets, candy, books, the list goes on . . . we are so grateful for the effort of thoughts, love, and kindness sent her way. She did look at us puzzled and asked, "Why would people buy me gifts?"

Since coming home, Caroline has been laughing, smiling, and following Matthew all around. She adores her big brother! I know God will use him in the process of her healing as well as her helping him through this difficult time. Matthew has really amazed me with his maturity in encouraging her and helping with the normalcy of life. He has been her rock!

We are getting into our daily routine of baths, cocoa butter massages, and therapy. And, oh boy... Momma's the nurse now. We've gotten tickled on Caroline's "beautiful" wrappings in her bandages. At one point she looked like a mummy with white gauze falling and flowing at her feet!

Caroline still amazes me, but I know it is God within her working out His plan! She has been smiling, laughing, hugging, playing, reading, enjoying her friends, riding her scooter (in air conditioning), and spreading the joy! One of her friends said to her mom, "She's the same Caroline! Nothing's changed, Mom."

It's Not Always Roses

Baths and massages are very painful for Caroline. But there are a lot of good things God is doing, and that's where we put our focus and energy: on all that God has and will do. The other day I walked in on a sweet conversation Caroline and my dad were having. He told her that God has given her grace, and she said, "Is that like sitting in His lap?" My eyes welled with tears; how simple, yet true.

Her brother continues to normalize life for her. Wherever Matthew is there is Caroline, being kids. He has a fun-filled summer planned and is looking forward to spending time with his friends.

Caroline and I had a wonderful visit with her kindergarten class last week. We were so happy to connect with her friends before the summer and answer any questions they might have. They wanted to be sure Caroline would be in first grade with them and would be able to run fast, swim, and play. That night, I thanked God for the school's teachers and staff. They truly exemplify the love of Christ.

The next day, a little smiley, big-brown-eyed girl poked her head in the kitchen door and asked if she could Hula-Hoop in her bedroom! "Yes, Caroline, go for it!" Because, let's see . . . you've roller skated in your bathroom, jumped off your bed thinking you were a spy going from building to building, ridden your Razor while saying you were getting the bad guys . . . Why not Hula-Hoop in the bedroom?

Caroline is doing well. However, we do understand what is meant by it being an up-and-down journey. Some days have been better than others, but we continue to make the best of the situation we are in.

The best medicine has been doing "normal" things that we have always done. She has especially enjoyed the sweet cards and pictures she has received from children all over the country. She continues to amaze us with her love of life and funny antics. In the days she has been home, I rejoice in having her here but struggle because sleep is nonexistent. I feel like a momma with a newborn . . . up every hour!

Life Is More Normal

In the months since Caroline's return, life has begun to return to normal. Matthew is doing well and growing into a preteen right before our eyes. I am in awe of his conversations with me, with his dreams and goals in life. He is much more mature than I was at ten. He has had a lot more to deal with in his short life, with his daddy's strokes and sister's accident.

Caroline's daddy is her best distraction during her skin massages and putting her splints on at night. They play Batman on the Xbox, make silly faces, play chase, wrestle, and snuggle. He has been such a strong encouragement to her.

More antics from Caroline: One night while Caroline is getting ready for bed, she says she can't wait to dance with Jesus and hug Him while listening to the song "I Can Only Imagine" over and over for hours (we can all now sing the song from memory!).

Another night she lines up her stuffed animals for a puppet show she produced and wrote. She says every funny line in the Alvin and the Chipmunks: Chipwrecked movie and sings every song (this so annoys Matthew).

Caroline's antics continue while at the doctor's office. She wore her 3-D glasses for her skin graft pictures. She posed for every picture, as the photographer laughed and said she had never had a patient bring props for her photo shoot in the burn unit! Then Caroline found the hospital gloves and put those on to add to her attire. Also, the doctor asked to inspect a certain area, and Caroline wiggled her booty at her.

We are in prayer about her right triceps. Caroline is not able to do certain activities with her right arm, like get her arm to her mouth or straighten her elbow on her own. Next week's tests will be run to see how much of her triceps muscle is missing due to the burns. I'm looking at her and saying, "She's alive, we can deal with this, and at least she has her arm."

Matthew is Caroline's rule keeper and marches through to be sure she is doing what she should be doing to get better. He's tougher on her than I am . . . which may be a good thing at times. He is really enjoying his summer and was so excited to be with his grandparents on a trip to Chattanooga. He also got to spend time with his cousins while there and be the center of attention. He even asked if he could live with his cousins for the summer.

Caroline Goes Back to School

After three months home, Caroline returned to school. I asked at breakfast the first day, "Are you ready for school?"

"No," she says. "I want to go to Mommy school."

I replied, "No, baby, you are headed to big school."

On the ride to school, Lamentations 3:22–24, came to mind: "Because of the Lord's great love we are not consumed, for his compassions never fail. They are new every morning; great is your faithfulness."

I continue to be amazed with God's healing hand and the outpouring of love from our family, friends, and new friends. I am especially thankful for our team of therapists. They are truly the most patient people I have ever met. They have been working diligently with Caroline and have provided such a fun atmosphere. Caroline loves them and hugs them every time she sees them.

Matthew is doing well—just a little upset his sis messed up his summer! Like I said, he normalizes life for her. He has been practicing soccer and enjoying new friends. We had a tournament where the accident happened and were apprehensive to go, but God reminded me, "This is the place where Caroline lived. I was there the whole time and sent my angels . . ."

This weekend my sweet husband is doing all the care for Caroline, to give me a break. What do I do? Sleep is on the agenda and spending quality time with Matthew. We talked for two hours straight last night while dribbling a soccer ball. I loved every minute of it. I love having a peek inside his heart.

While at therapy one day, Caroline had my phone in the bathroom with her. It was taking her quite a while, so I knocked and asked if she needed my help. At which she replied, "No."

Later, upon arriving home, I checked my messages and realized Caroline had taken a video of her toes while sitting on the potty. They were getting married. However, in her hearing of marriage vows she thought they were saying, "Do you take this awful husband to be your awful husband?" "I do!" "And do you take this awful wife to be your awful wife?" "I do!" Then her big toes kissed.

When I told my family what had happened, my dad asked Caroline, "Well, did you go potty?" She replied, "No."

Caroline does not care what she wears. We went to Arby's the other day, and she wore her polka-dot white bathrobe. "Caroline, do you have anything underneath your robe?" I asked.

"It's not a robe, Mommy! It's a karate girl costume!"

Depths of His Grace

"Your grace still amazes me. Your love is a mystery... I fall on my knees." These were the words so beautifully sung at our church on Sunday. God gently brought them to mind again today, of the depth of His love and His grace that is incomprehensible. I am so humbled and overwhelmed by His love and grace.

Caroline had her muscle/nerve tests today. Results were normal! The doctor used that word again: "miracle." Electrical burns can cause a problem with nerves firing. Caroline's were all within normal range.

We were grateful for God's outcome, but the tests were very painful and difficult for Caroline. It took over two hours . . . with a momma drenched, literally, from head to toe in sweat. We are exhausted.

She Is Alive!

"Boo!" shouted a bright-eyed, six-year-old girl!

"Boo!" I shouted back as I ran to tackle and tickle this precious little girl.

It's hard to believe that just five months ago today Caroline had her accident. Life as we knew it changed. God reached down in His grace and mercy and did what seemed impossible and made it possible. She is alive! And for that, we are so grateful.

Her zest and zeal for life is so contagious that it touches those around her, including her brother, who says she can be so annoying with her jumping and singing and dancing and flowers and butterflies and talking nonstop and smiling. He pleads, "Mom, can you please tell Caroline to stop talking? My brain can't handle all of this. I have a headache."

I tell him God's preparing him for his future wife, as he slyly rolls his eyes and grins at me.

Caroline is literally dancing and singing her way through life. She attends first grade every day and even has special treats from a sweet and caring little boy in her class. One such day Caroline was hot, so he made her a paper fan to cool herself. Another day he made a rainbow-colored hairband necklace and a hairband "BFF" (best friends forever) bracelet. She wears one of them every day.

Yes, I told her, he's a "keeper."

"What's a keeper, Mom?"

Therapy is twice a week. Her arm and elbow are doing well but will need constant stretching to gain full range of movement. Some days are better than others. Caroline has declared she wants to try cheering (a two-day clinic). She said it would help her arm.

Matthew continues to be a wonderful big brother to Caroline, while also providing the normalcy in her life as he plays video games with her. He is coaching her in soccer and teaches her about life. They even have their own little secrets they share with each other. I love seeing their relationship flourish and grow. I hope and pray they can be best friends and provide the shoulder to lean on when life throws curve balls.

While chatting with Matthew about life, I have been amazed at his maturity and his love for God and doing the right thing. I love seeing into the windows of his heart. He is such a good guy. School is going well but proving to be quite a challenge in getting all his work done with our "not normal" lives. He is also enjoying soccer and making new friends. He has come out of his shell more and has courageously tackled issues that have not been easy. He is learning to persevere even when disappointments arise. This is a tough lesson to learn at ten, but I know God has something special in mind for Matthew.

Caroline continues her antics. She lost her first tooth, and the tooth fairy gave her more money than I ever received. Caroline had left a note under her pillow for the tooth fairy, asking her where she gets all her money. "Is it from God?" Already knows who owns it all? We don't know why but anytime Caroline says bye to someone she wiggles her booty and laughs. I've tried to tell her a hug and wave goodbye are just fine... no booty needed.

One night after one of Matthew's soccer games, Caroline jumped in the door to our house and announced, "Party in the house!"

Oh, dear Lord, what will she be like when she's a teenager?

Caroline gets ready for school to a different beat; just ask Matthew. "Mom, Caroline acts like it's a party to get ready for school. Her music is so loud, and she is dancing as she gets dressed! Mom, you need to talk to her and do something about this." Tell her to not enjoy life as much? She enjoys it all. I never want her to lose her zest for life, for people like her are the ones who make us smile and stop and enjoy life too. Thank you.

The other night while putting Caroline to bed, she and I prayed, as we do every night, but this time she grabbed both of my hands and closed her eyes so tight as she whispered, "Jesus, please heal my burns..."

Prayer, the First Line of Defense

Philip Wilson

The function of prayer is not to influence God, but rather to change the nature of the one who prays.

Søren Kierkegaard

DO YOU EVER WONDER IF God hears your prayers? Christians want to know their prayers are making a difference. If God knows our minds and what we need better than we ourselves do, should we even bother to pray? Why do we need to be involved? The Bible tells us God knows the number of hairs on our heads. When you pray, you are not informing God of anything he does not already know. So why did he tell us to do it?

Prayer is a difficult yet important part of the Christian life. God invites us to pray. His command to pray is the basis for why we need to pray. Jesus, God in human form, set the example. We pray because He told us to. He is God and we are not.

or listen!

Prayer is an awesome idea by itself. Human beings are able to talk to God, the creator of the universe, at any time or place. How cool is it that we can invite our creator to walk with us through life. Even if you pray only during trials, you acknowledge God as the sovereign controller of your life. He is the source who loves us, and we can call on him for help in times of trouble. Is there a certain way to pray that increases our chance of certain outcomes? Is there something we say or believe that makes our prayers more effective? What are the hindrances to effective prayer?

There are several ways to make prayer more powerful:
- First, identify and communicate the desire honestly (we must pray for our prayers to be heard!)
- Pray to God boldly.
- Release the problems.

- Have faithful confidence in the prayers.
- Pray with a clean heart.
- How we posture for prayer

"You have not because you ask not" (James 4:2). Maybe our life is in such turmoil because we ignore prayer? How many times do we pray for guidance before doing something important versus going to God to figure out our mess? God cares about all concerns and requests to share our lives. We ought to pray about everything, yet we tend to pray only in a crisis.

For us to have a real relationship, we need to invite God into our daily lives. Pray continually, not only in crisis or when we want something. Pray at all times, knowing God will answer, in His own time, and in His own way, not just when we are in need of a miracle.

The Bible talks about prayer without ceasing. Does that mean we are to go around all day praying? Prayer without ceasing means to live in a constant relationship with God. For example, in a good marriage you are able to approach your spouse about anything, at any time. You desire to invite a spouse into your life. You want to share your life with him or her. There is always a sense of presence. Conversation and companionship are natural.

The ultimate purpose of prayer is to be dependent upon God. Prayer is not for God's good but ours. Because God is who He is, He does not need our prayers. We need to pray. When we pray we acknowledge God's position in our lives. Dependence comes from acknowledging God answers yes, no, or wait. We are not in charge. We might pray, "This is what I would like to have happen, but I don't need it to be happy. You know what is best. I yield to Your will."

The answer is sometimes yes, sometimes no. There are times when God's purpose is set and has already determined the outcome, but in prayer, we acknowledge God's right to say no. Would it not be nice when our kids come to us with a request if they would respond positively and with acceptance when we say no? I hate the rolling eyes. What if they asked recognizing our right to say no?

When we say no it is not because we don't want to do things for them. Most of the time, it is for their benefit, even if they cannot see that.

Another common hindrance to prayer is not going to God boldly. We are taught God is a rewarder for those who seek him, yet many of us are uncertain about the power of prayer and our right to seek God. We have the authority to bring heaven to earth. God wants us to pray confident prayers. We are His children and He seeks a relationship with us.

What kind of prayers are you offering? Are you praying for God to change circumstances or to change you? When you pray, do you focus only on your daily wish list for God to fix, or do you focus on God? Is it always "give me, fix this, change that," or is it "make me into what you want me to be"? We need to discipline ourselves to go to God with the same fever (boldness) as we bring to God when problems are choking us.

We approach God in friendship. Effective prayer is influenced by our relationship with God. The depth and strength of our prayer life are directly related to the depth and strength of our personal relationship with Him. Don't be ashamed to beg God for a miracle. If you needed something, would you hide that from a friend? Thank God ahead of time for meeting our unmet needs. Thanking God ahead of meeting needs shows trust. If you walk with Him and trust Him in advance for how He answers, you are trusting Him for what is best in your life.

Another hindrance to prayer is how we release our problems. Do you truly cast your cares, asking God to take over your circumstances, or do you continue to stare at the problem? Do you believe prayer is the best way to handle problems?

One way to tell if you are truly releasing your problems to God is to note whether you are still worrying or thinking about them. If you have done your part, trusted God to do what you cannot do, then why are you worried? This is the God who created the universe; don't you think he can solve your "little" problem? Prayer should be our first response to a problem, not the last one for when you have exhausted everything else. When we are prompted to pray, we should pray immediately; not after we have exhausted all other avenues and are desperate.

74

Yet another hindrance is not having confidence in your prayers. I know at times in my life I have questioned this: Why would God care about that little thing? You can ask for anything, while trusting God even if He says no. The attitude is that we ask Him thankfully, knowing in advance, He will answer in His time. We thank Him in advance for the answer that is on the way.

It is a hindrance when we pray without a clean heart. The prayers of a righteous man are more effective. Proverbs 10:24 states, "the wicked dread will overtake them; what the righteous desire will be granted."

In the Bible, Elijah prayed earnestly that it would not rain, and it did not rain on the land for three and a half years. Again he prayed, and the heavens gave rain, and the earth produced its crops. This does not mean that you need to shout or weep or moan. All is needed is a simple heartfelt petition of God from a righteous person.

Also in the Bible is the story of Hezekiah. He became the king of Jerusalem when he was twenty-five years old and ruled for twenty-nine years. The Scripture says he was pleasing in God's sight because he remained faithful in everything. He became sick and prayed to God to extend his life, and God did. Did God know Hezekiah's prayer before he prayed it, and how He would answer? The answer to both questions is yes. Prayer does not change God's mind in the way we think of it. God knows the future and we don't. Hezekiah did not know how God would answer. He did not know his prayer before he made it. Prayer is important to living out God's will every day. Does prayer change God's mind? No. Does prayer change things? Yes. It is *the primary means by which God brings our will into harmony with His will.*

There are certain things we cannot change. God's mind was set for sending Jesus to bring salvation. Had we prayed not to send Jesus, it would not have mattered. God has decreed certain events since before the world was created, and it is inevitable that they will come to pass.

The mind of God does not change, because God does not change. Things change according to his sovereign will. However, his sovereign will is worked out through secondary means and secondary activities. Prayer is one of those secondary activities. We do change things within God's limits. Scripture is clear that without prayers we are not able to change anything.

When Jesus prayed in the garden, he asked God for the cup to be passed from Him. He requested this yet ultimately bowed to God's will for his life. We pray because we have an ability to change things within His limits. We are allowed to reorder things according to his purpose.

Should I bother God with the little things in my life or leave Him alone and focus on executing His will if it is best for my life anyway? The answer is found when you look at the example of Jesus. He knew the wisdom of His heavenly father, yet He constantly prayed. Prayer is not a means of removing the unknown elements in life, but rather a way of including ourselves in the working out of His will in our lives. Prayer affects the person praying.

A common hindrance to prayer is how we posture for our prayers. The Bible does not give a required posture for praying. We are told only that we can pray anytime and in any place. Some Christians tend to make this too religious, thinking there should be a certain posture or certain words for God to hear our prayer. Sometimes we think prayer needs to be for a certain period of time. It is conversation. How do you talk to your friends? Do you talk to God like a friend?

I know my own biggest hindrance is my mind wandering during prayer. I have trouble quieting my mind to focus. It is almost like subtle spiritual warfare, as if the Devil is trying to pull me away from talking to God. Consider this idea: Start praying, and when your mind starts wandering, pick up a Bible and read. Once focused, start praying again; and repeat if necessary.

Jesus also talked about how we should pray. The first priority of our prayers should be to declare God's greatness and surrender to His will. Then petition for needs. We don't need to start our prayers by asking. Prayer is not a means to bend God's will to ours. The purpose of prayer is surrendering our will to His.

Beyond Human Limitations

By Philip Wilson

Grace is the power of the Holy Spirit coming to us free of charge to enable you to do with ease what you could never do on your own with any amount of struggle and effort. Joyce Meyer

THE BIBLE PROMISES THAT WHEN you accept Jesus Christ as your Savior, you become born again. Once born again, you receive the power of God. The power of God lives inside of you in the form of the Holy Spirit. Do you feel like you have the power of God inside of you?

I think most people would answer "no" or "I am not sure." If your answer is one of these, then either the Bible is not true and you never received God's Spirit when saved or you must be doing something to disconnect the power.

The power of the Holy Spirit is given to us so that we can do things that we cannot do by ourselves. It is enabling power available to us as a guide to make decisions, and it sustains us in times of need. It is the power of God available to believers to strengthen us through our storms. The Holy Spirit is sometimes called the Great Comforter, because of how it helps us through difficult times.

When people do not feel the power of God, it is usually for several reasons:
- Living with known sin.
- Not being led by peace.
- Not developing the daily disciplines.
- Being too busy.

Imagine what the world would be like if everyone was filled with the Holy Spirit. Imagine what our lives would be like if we tapped the power of God. If you asked people if they would like to have the power of God inside of them to direct their steps, most would answer, "Absolutely!"

Our ability to access God's power begins with an understanding of the conditions necessary for the Holy Spirit to work inside of us. The first necessary condition is to be saved. The Holy Spirit is available only to those who have accepted Jesus Christ as their Savior.

The next condition needed for the Holy Spirit to operate is to be cleansed. To be Spirit-filled, you cannot have known sin in your life. One job of the Holy Spirit is convicting us of our sins and showing us the need for forgiveness. You must be right with God. Since we all sin, we must continually repent. To repent means to ask for forgiveness and turn in another direction. Repentance implies a change in conduct. Being right with God means living according to God's will for your life, not your own. When you sin and fall short, you repent and get right with Him.

The next necessary condition is obedience. If you want to hear from God, you first must learn how to obey what He has already told you to do. It is easy to say you want God to speak to you, but if you are really listening only when it is what you want to hear, obeying only what you find is convenient, you will be disconnected from His power. Why would God continue to give you guidance for your life if you don't follow His last leading He gave you? Why would He tell you anything new if you did not do the last thing He told you? Hear and obey.

Do you ever feel you are struggling to do something? If so, most of the time it is because you are trying to do something only God can do. You have stepped outside His will for your life. Most of our frustrations during storms come from when we are trying to take action to change circumstances when there is nothing we can do. John 15:5 says, "I am the vine; you are the branches. If you remain in me and I in you, you will bear much fruit; apart from me you can do nothing."

78

When you find yourself in a struggle to do something, it is often because you are cut off from the vine. Be honest. It is not always easy to do the right thing or to follow God's will. God does not expect you to be perfect in order to be connected to Him, but you are not going to hear from God if you are living for yourself.

Often believers do not feel the power of God inside of them because they are unable to be led by peace. The power of God is not necessarily the same kind of power that we are often used to. We serve a big God. Certainly God can do miraculous things, but He often leads us by peace, not a miraculous sign. Our revelations often come to us as a calmness we feel inside of us.

For example, if a single person asked me how I knew Rhonda was the one for me to marry, I would answer, "I didn't." I thought she was, but I was not sure. But when I decided to offer her a ring, it just felt natural. I was at peace. You can never know everything about your spouse before you get married. But I just had peace about the decision. I remember the day of my wedding walking up to the altar with the minister. It felt right. I was calm even though I was about to make a decision that was for life.

When you are led by peace, you are operating in the will of God. One way to know it is not God's will is that you do not feel at peace about it; it is probably something you should not do. God often leads us with a restless spirit. In your heart you feel that tug, as if God was trying to get your attention. Difference in Fear

To be filled with the Holy Spirit, we need to develop the daily disciplines of prayer and Bible study. The Holy Spirit is the living presence of God. The Bible talks about "setting your mind on things above." We have to continually renew our mind, which is done through the daily disciplines. God releases His power to us while we are engaged in the daily disciplines. We often don't feel His presence because we are not engaged in regular prayer and study. If you spend several hours in front of the TV everyday but just a few minutes reading and studying the Bible, it is not surprising you don't feel the power. The more we spend time with God, the more our minds are filled with His Spirit; otherwise, worldly thinking will overpower our minds.

Are you busy or fruitful? One of the Holy Spirit's jobs is to help us live out God's will in our lives. The Bible refers to God as the "still, small voice." Are you having trouble hearing from God and accessing His power because you are too busy? Sometimes all we need to do is slow down.

If you feel you are too busy, change the way you look at the problem. The problem with feeling you are too busy often is not a time management problem. There just is not enough time to handle everything.

You have to cut out some things. We all seem to know that, but we don't want to disappoint anyone. Even if we know reducing obligations to others is the right thing to do, we must accept that somebody is going to be disappointed. We have to have limits. We must decide who is going to miss out. When we strain to keep everyone happy, we will end up making someone unhappy that we would rather not, like a spouse.

What does it look like when you are Spirit-filled? Spirit-filled believers radiate praise and thanksgiving to God. They have submitted their lives to the great change agent and cannot wait to be amazed by what God is going to do. Their lives have purpose. They believe God is in charge and that His plan is best for their lives. A Spirit-filled believer has the power of God, which enables him or her to do things beyond human limitations.

The Word "Christian" is an Adjective, Not a Noun

Philip Wilson

Just because you go to church doesn't mean you're a Christian. I can go sit in the garage all day and it doesn't make me a car.

Joyce Meyer

GROWING UP IN A CHURCH, I was often confused by what it meant to be Christian. Notice I did not say "a Christian" but "Christian." Most people identify being a Christian with going to church. As I have grown older, I have learned that is not necessarily the case. In fact, seeing others at church whose lives show little difference from those that go to church and profess to be a Christian is a big reason why many people don't go to church.

What is the point, if they just act like everyone else? Churchgoers are sometimes no better than the rest of the world, but often come across as if they are. Jesus did not die because we were perfect or even deserving. Jesus did not die so we could have a religion. He died for us to have a relationship.

Our relationship is based on our own belief that we are not worthy. Without Him our lives are a mess. I am really bothered by the Christian checklist mentality: carry your Bible, go to church, and tell others how much you pray. A list of "religious" activities that, if you do them, means you are a "serious" Christian.

This type of thinking is the very thing Jesus condemned while here on earth. Jesus spent time with losers, thieves, adulterers, and many others considered "less worthy" by the Jewish leaders of the time. Jesus seemed to be attracted to the "less worthy" because they were the ones who were a mess and needed saving. The Pharisees were too proud to think they needed salvation.

The Bible does not define the word "Christian." In fact, it does not even use the word. It is our word. The word the Bible uses is disciple. A disciple is someone who follows the teachings of Jesus. Sometimes churchgoers' minds are so full of information that they can focus only on spiritual knowledge, not on obedience. The true test for a Christian is not to teach others how much you know, but to live what you know and let others see it.

We cannot love other people when we are thinking we are more important or better. Our worth and value comes from God. God is impressed by what we do, not by what we say. He is not impressed when we think we are better than others.

If you believe in God, you believe you were created by Him and that your life has a purpose. The purpose is to bring God glory. God finds pleasure when we truly understand our purpose and our significance. *How bring glory by obeying what greatest command? LOVE - our purpose = Love*

I am amazed at how many men doubt their life has a purpose. The focus is on their work and doing something they enjoy. Serving God is not always fun. Bringing God glory is not always fun. Your purpose is to bring God pleasure, not to bring yourself pleasure. God put you where you are. You need to be faithful and focus on bringing *LOVE* God glory where you are today and not on where you want to be a few years from now. Allow God to use you right where you are. This type of thought process directly affects how we manage storms.

I am amazed when women say, "I am just a stay-at-home mom." What a pitiful response to your purpose. Raising children is a high calling. God does not think any better of a brain surgeon than of a mom who wipes bottoms. We bring God glory by being a good manager of where we are right now.

Bringing glory to God is what this book is all about. We bring the greatest amount of glory to God in how we handle our storms. Storms change us. They make us valuable in His kingdom. They show the world and ourselves that He is in charge.

Think about what it means to be a disciple next time you have a storm. Remember your high calling. Remember your purpose. Remember why you are here. You were created by God for an eternal relationship with God. In God, we find our meaning, our purpose, our strength. Without God we have nothing and are nothing. *love*

The word Christian is a description of a way of life. It is not some checklist of items we cross off to be called worthy. The opposite is true. No matter what we do, we are not worthy. Everyone sins. We are all screw-ups. We all suffer from the same problem. Our sin separates us from God. Therefore, it separates us from our purpose.

I know that many of the people who will read this book are hurting. They are unable to press past the pain, and they are miserable because of it. Give it to God. In Him, and only in Him do we find our purpose, our meaning. Our high calling is for an eternal relationship with God through Jesus Christ. It is only there we find the strength to press through the storm.

More Help Moving Past "Why"

Philip Wilson

Only a life lived for others is a life worthwhile.
Albert Einstein

IF WE ARE ABLE TO move forward with God, we must learn how to put the "why" aside and focus forward. I have found a few helpful ways to do this:

- leaning on your spouse
- worship
- helping others
- remembering God's promises

Marriage is a gift from God to glorify Him. Spouses and friends can be quite helpful in dealing with storms. However, men seem to avoid discussing problems because they view it as a weakness. We men seem to pride ourselves on solving problems and being self-sufficient. We need help to work through difficult issues, and must resist the urge to try to deal with everything without help. Put aside the pride.

In my marriage, I have always needed help from my wife to work through issues but sometimes have trouble asking. I take a lot of pride in being self-sufficient, but my wife is a wonderful listener and brings a different perspective to issues. Even if she does not solve the problem, her insight is helpful to me to work through the issues.

There is a reason God put men and women together. We were not meant to go it alone. Open up to your spouse. Give her the opportunity to help you work through storms.

Women need the counsel of their spouses just as much as men need their wives. Men can help women to work through their feelings by bringing a grounded, less-emotional perspective to problems. One tip I learned in my marriage is to listen and try not to speak. Men rush to a solution too quickly. Even though you may understand the problem and know how to solve it, men just need to zip it and listen. Women often just want understanding and empathy.

For the women readers, there are some basic tips I can give you about men. The first is that when a man does not want to talk about an issue, you are not going to get him to talk by pushing for him to share more or pressing for more of a discussion. Men talk when they're ready. My wife understands the "cave." The cave is that safe place that men withdraw to when they need time away from the problems of the world. It may take the form of reading the paper, watching TV, or exercising, but wives need to realize that when a man is in his cave, he is not going to come out until he is ready. Men are like rubber bands. They pull away but will snap back in their own time.

Also, when a man gets home from work, be careful not to unload the day's problems on him. Give him some time to retreat to the cave before doing so. I think you will find he listens better to you and opens up more when you do this, especially if you create the right atmosphere (safer) for men to share.

Remember women and men are not alike. Their needs are very different. Men need respect. Women need to accept men's need for respect and meet it. Do not shame men for how they were created. Tell your husband often you respect him. Men want to have a wife that is proud of them.

From my experience, women need to hear they are beautiful. I have never heard of anyone who said they were tired of hearing that. Tell your wife if you had to do it all over again, you would not think twice about marrying her again. Women need to hear words of security. This is what draws them back to you. A little tip for the men, women like you to check in with them during the day, just to let them know you are thinking about them. I used to think my wife was being nosy about details of my day, when all she really wanted to do was connect.

Both spouses need to be careful not to place conditions on your affections. *Well, I would do more of that, if he would just do more of this.* If she was just this, then I would be more receptive to that. And be careful about what you think and say about your spouse, especially to friends and family. Talk and focus on the good things your spouse does. When you focus on the good you will draw out more of the good. Don't withhold anything. Men need to talk more than they want to. Don't withhold what your spouse needs because you are upset about something else.

Worship is helpful for moving past "why." In the dictionary, worship is defined as "reverent honor paid to God." When we worship, something happens inside us. God seems to strengthen and comfort us in times of worship. The Bible does not define worship, but it does say we need to praise God. We should honor and thank Him for what He has done, is doing, and will do. We worship God for who He is and acknowledge His character.

The first time worship is mentioned in the Bible is with Abraham. Abraham was a man who showed us great faith and he is described as a friend of God. He was asked by God to give Him his beloved son Issac. Abraham obeyed, showing God he would not withhold anything from Him. Think of your storms as opportunities to show God He is first place. *Offering your suffering as a means of worship shows God He is in control.*

Worship is more than just going to church. Church worship is important for the believer. I find that God talks to me more in that setting than any other, often through the sermon, through music, or just in talking to someone. But going to Church is not necessary for worship.

Sometimes people going through trials avoid church, because they don't want to be reminded of their issues or talk about them with others. Sometimes this is because church members can say the wrong thing and pry too much. If this is something you fear will happen, go see your pastor in private. Pastors are some of the most gifted and wisest persons on the planet.

← not just $

Worship involves all aspects of your life, especially giving. Tithing and offerings are a powerful part of worship. When we give, we recognize God's ownership in our financial lives. We are recognizing God owns it all, and we are obediently returning a portion to him. This is a form of worship. Open up your wallet, you will find you shrink your storms. Just like Abraham, show God He is first. I am not suggesting that we need to sacrifice (like Abraham) our children. But giving is worship. Sacrificing is worship. Give until it hurts. Give what you cannot afford to give. *We are never more like Jesus than when we are a sacrificial giver.*

Are you always on your mind? Do you struggle moving forward because of self-pity? Have you ever noticed some of the happiest, most peaceful people you see stay busy helping others? Activity minimizes self-pity. When you pour into the lives of others and bear their burdens, your troubles don't seem so large. "Carry each other's burdens, and in this way you will fulfill the law of Christ" (Galatians 6:2).

Find the one

We are all so self-involved. Get your focus off yourself. Take time to meet the needs of someone else. Wake up with a mind-set of "Who can I bless today?" rather than "Who is going to bless me?" We are blessed by being a blessing to others. You were built by God in His image, and He is a giver. We should be also.

I have found that God meets my needs in abundance when I meet the needs of others. I am not saying you can manipulate God's favor on you by helping someone else. Maybe it is just that when we have a consistent focus on others (not ourselves), it is easier for us to see how our needs are being met. Maybe it is just easier to see God working in our lives.

The will of God is to be thankful in all circumstances. When we retreat to the world of feeling sorry for ourselves, we are rebelling against God. When we are busy and not sitting around, it is difficult for the Devil to mess with our thoughts. We have to make a conscious decision to get off the couch and get busy in the lives of others. We don't have to look very far to find a worthy cause. Open your eyes, listen for the Holy Spirit to lead you to people in need. Be a blessing to others. God is looking for people to work through. We need to spend more time looking to be a blessing instead of being blessed.

87

It is helpful to move past "why" by repeating God's promises. When we do this, God's promises are internalized, and we are able to act as we would when not in a storm. They are branded on our hearts, and our faith is increased.

Here are some powerful verses for your storm moments:

"And let us not lose heart and grow weary and faint acting nobly and doing right, for in due time and at season we shall reap, if we do not loosen and relax our courage and faint." (Galatians 6:9)

"One thing I do is forgetting what lies behind and press forward to what lies ahead." (Phil 3:13)

"Take my yoke upon you and learn from me, for I am gentle and humble in heart and you will find rest for your souls." (Matthew 11:29)

"Finally, be strong in the Lord and in his mighty power. Put on the full armor of God so you can take your stand against the devil's schemes." (Eph 6:10–11)

"Be self-controlled and alert. Your enemy, the devil, prowls around like a roaring lion looking for someone to devour. Resist him and stand firm in your faith because you know your brothers throughout the world are undergoing the same kind of sufferings. And the God of all grace, who called you to his eternal glory in Christ, after you have suffered a little while, will himself restore you and make you strong, firm, and steadfast." (1 Peter 5:8–10)

"No temptation has overtaken you that is not common to man. God is faithful, and he will not let you be tempted beyond your ability, but with the temptation he will also provide the way of escape, that you may be able to endure it." (1 Corinthians 10:13)

"Blessed is the man who remains steadfast under trial, for when he has stood the test he will receive the crown of life, which God has promised to those who love him." (James 1:12)

"I can do all things through him who strengthens me." (Philippians 4:13)

"For his anger lasts only a moment, but his favor last a lifetime; weeping may remain for a night, but rejoicing comes in the morning." (Psalm 30:5)

"Do not be anxious about anything, but in every situation, by prayer and petition, with thanksgiving, present your requests to God. And the peace of God, which transcends all understanding, will guard your hearts and your minds in Christ Jesus." (Philippians 4:6–7)

How to Help Others Going through a Storm

Philip and Rhonda Wilson

Our human compassion binds us the one to the other—not in pity or patronizingly, but as human beings who have learned how to turn our common suffering into hope for the future. Nelson Mandela

WHEN WE ARE IN THE midst of the storm, so many people and family members want to help and support us in any way they can, but help needs to come in the right way. Here are four very helpful things to consider:

- praying
- sending gifts
- leaving encouraging messages, texts
- providing meals

Praying for the family and those in crisis mode is the most important thing a person can do to help. During my husband's strokes and Caroline's hospital stay, people often asked, "What can I do? What is the best way for me to help you?" I simply said, "Pray." During our storms, we felt those prayers and are forever grateful for them, because those are what got us through those hard times. Another helpful and touching thing to do is to send a card, flowers, gift, or something to let the family know you are thinking about them and love them. It is so touching when people take time out of their day to do this. These expressions of God's love reap bountifully and encourage the family to press on while also providing smiles where tears once were.

You can also reach out to those in the storm by leaving voice messages, e-mails, or texts—let them know you love and care and are there to help. We cannot tell you the number of people who reached out with texting devotionals or prayers. This was such a blessing to our hearts and encouragement to our souls. However, be careful not to ask for a return phone call or response. Let loved ones in suffering know you are thinking of them, but do not ask for anything of them (like an update).

When encouraging others, be careful not to impose on them for information. A person going through a storm is overwhelmed. Reporting events of the day to others is exhausting. You don't need to know a play-by-play to help them. Offer to listen if someone wants to talk; don't make them feel an obligation to keep you informed.

Say or text something like, "I can only imagine you are overwhelmed, I just want you to know I love you and are praying for you, so please do not feel like you have to call me back. But if you would like to talk, I am here."

If you do talk with someone going through a storm, be careful not to feed their worry with, "What are you going to do?" I know you may think it is useful to help someone process a situation, but it can work against God. How can a person cast their cares on God and let Him lead their steps, if everyone around them is asking them their next move?

Providing healthful meals can be such a tremendous help to the one in the storm. To not have to go to the grocery store and plan meals was such a weight lifted off our shoulders. It allowed us to focus our energy and efforts on Caroline and Matthew.

Other things can cause a burden for those in the storms. We hate to admit, we have done some of these things, thinking we were offering an ear to listen or providing support when really we were being more of a burden!

When supporting others through a storm, there are several important things to remember:
- Try not to take control.
- Allow grace for those in the storms.
- Do not expect updates.
- Shorten your visits

Be careful not to take control of the crisis even if your intentions are good, even if what you think needs to happen should happen. Life is out of control for the ones in the storm, so do not take it upon yourself to decide for them what is best. Help where needed, such as providing moral support, a listening ear, and "manpower." But respectfully allow the important decisions to be made by those in the storm.

Be mindful that *your desire to control a situation may be a solution to your own anxiety*, not necessarily in the best interest for those going through the storms; too many chiefs in the camp courts disaster. When Caroline was in the hospital, several times friends and family were actually working against us while trying to help us. They meant well but did not have all the information we had to make the best decision, or maybe we did not want to hurt their feelings by telling them that we did not want to do what they wanted. In some of those occasions, we were actually criticized and pressured for the decisions we made together because others did not agree with them.

Allow grace. Those in the storms will not be on their best behavior, due to the stress of the event, lack of sleep and food, and anxieties about the unknowns. Allow grace to prevail when darts of anger come your way or weariness of the heart cannot be helped. Don't take it personally, but realize their lives are upside down. Expecting normal behavior from a person going through a storm is not fair to that person.

Again, do not continue to ask for updates. I know that's hard, but calling and e-mailing for updates is just another thing the person in the storm feels like they have to do. Life has thrown them a curve ball of chaos, so allow them to update you in ways such as social networking sites. Again, let them know you care, but do not make demands on them.

We were warned by pastors and crisis personnel to be careful about the stress that people can place on you. It is hard not to be a burden on those going through storms. *Sometimes when we ask for updates, are really trying to alleviate our own anxieties.*

We realized this when we contrasted our experiences at the Mayo Clinic with Caroline's stay at Children's Hospital. At the Mayo Clinic there was no one around. We were in another state. Caroline's accident was much more exhausting, in part because of so many around us. We appreciated the love and concern shown to us during that time. But we were exhausted. The hospital was rough. Sometimes people would come to see us but leave hurt because we were not able to greet them. Sometimes we were unavailable because we were providing care to Caroline. Other times, we were just exhausted and did not want to play host to visitors and answer and discuss our situation, yet again, with someone else. We loved the visitors and realized their questions and concerns were out of love and sincere desire to help, but we were always exhausted and very busy all day.

Oftentimes when people were not visiting, we would try to catch a catnap so we could be fresh for whatever the day held. Most people typically visit during the day. A better time to visit would be on the weekends because there are less things going on (less doctor visits, less therapy, etc.) and the patient is more rested. Another idea is to put a book people can sign and leave an encouraging note at the front desk. How we loved to read the book to Caroline, and tell her about whom the person was and our relationship to them.

Be careful that you are not just trying to be the "inside" friend who has access to the updates and the latest news. Most people going through a storm will want to talk, but only to a small number of people. Who they choose to talk with does not reflect on your friendship or how important you are to them. Remember, you are not the only person asking for updates and calling to check on them. When visiting, be careful not to overstay your visit. While visiting and providing moral support are very helpful, remember that you are not the only person who came to visit that day. The best thing to do is call or e-mail that you would like to come by to see them and ask if such-and-such a time would be good. *Let the person you are visiting make that decision about the details and time of the visit.* Give them the ability to decline the visit without it being awkward.

Please don't misunderstand. The outpouring we receive from others, I think, is part of the way God strengthens us through tough times. But when you are a patient, those small visits exhaust you. The patient is often embarrassed, because there are tubes sticking out of everything. People in hospitals generally have not showered and have to wear those revealing hospital gowns. It can be embarrassing for friends to see you at your worst. Think about the last time you were sick with the flu or some type of bug. You just wanted to sleep, not answer questions like "how do you feel?"

Some people are introverts (like Philip) and don't want a lot of people around. Some people are extraverts (like Rhonda) and are energized by having people around. But if you are respectful of people's wishes, everyone is happy. Do not take it upon yourself to decide what is best for the people involved.

We really believe that, in part, Philip's miraculous recovery after the strokes was because he was 100 percent focused on his therapy. We were so exhausted all day and it would have been difficult to "put on" the good face if people had visited. Philip could not talk. It would have been embarrassing for him to see people. Introverts are not energized by having people around. We believe had he had a lot of visitors, his energy would have diminished his ability to have successful therapy. Therapy required so much energy mentally and physically. When he was not in therapy, he was resting.

You can be an incredible encourager to others going through a storm. Show others God's love—just be mindful of how and when it is done.

Helping Children through the Storm

Rhonda Wilson

Human beings are the only creatures that allow their children to come back home.
Bill Cosby

TRAUMATIC EXPERIENCE CAN BE CHALLENGING enough for an adult, but to a child in the storm it can be a place of uncertainty, fear, and insecurity. Their world has been rocked. Philip and I learned a thing or two about guiding children through the storm. Yes, they can feel all the emotions and insecurities we face as adults, but they don't know how to cope. Traumatic experiences affect children and it is our job as parents and adults to guide them through the process of loss and grief.

Grieving may come to a child in the form of a loss of a parent (not just by death, but through separation or divorce as well), loss of a pet, loss of a special toy, a move to another school, or death of a friend or family member. They will look to us for how we handle loss. Do we stuff our feelings? Do we pretend all is okay in our world? Do we grieve and move on? What does our body language convey to our children?

We are often grieving as well, but confusion has entered the child's world. So how do we encourage them to move past the hurts and find security in the One who created them? We have learned several principles to help children in the midst of grief.

Losses to both children and adults are the death of a dream and expectations that life will remain as it is. One of the most important reassurances to a grieving child is to know they are <u>fully and unconditionally loved</u>. Your love for them has and always will remain the same, even though life has taken a turn in their world of security. This assurance that your relationship will never change provides them a valuable sense of love and security. The warmth of your embrace, a word of encouragement, and the words "I love you" are very important in showing them you still love and care for them. Say it often. Children never tire of hearing it or that you are proud of them.

Some ways Philip and I continued to reassure Matthew of our love for him were to spend time playing with him and being a presence at his activities both at school and at soccer. Yes, things had changed in our worlds. But our love for Matthew did not change. Lots of hugs and kisses were doled out to him as well!

When Caroline was in the hospital, Philip was with her all day. When he got home at night, he consciously tried to have quality time with Matthew. This is not easy when you are tired, but he would try to do something special, like playing games, wrestling, or watching a movie.

Another important aspect of helping children through the storms is to keep their routine. This is not always an easy task, but trying to remain on the same schedule as much as possible will help provide a sense of security to children.

Believe it or not, Matthew and I decided for him to go to school the day after the accident! We both felt this would be best for him and provide a sense of normalcy in the midst of chaos. We were also blessed to have grandparents take an active role in helping to provide stability and security. Staying at our home to keep Matthew in his element and on his schedule proved to be healing for him and diminished anxiety. This also provided Matthew with a sense of security: even though our world had changed, our love for him had not.

Philip and I also found that children who are grieving need the safe environment of a listening ear, an environment where they can express their anger, hurts, fears, and insecurities of their changing world. Listening to their hearts provides you a window into their thoughts and a safe place for them to express their confusion and fears without judgment. We have found this to be a very important tool in helping children work through their emotions and move on from the hurts of life.

Oftentimes after Caroline's accident, I lay across Matthew's bed and said nothing. Yes, I just lay there motionless, with a zipped mouth. And a few minutes later our child would share his heart about anything and everything. Sometimes the accident wasn't even mentioned in his bouts of chatting. Whatever was on his heart at that moment is what was important to listen to. Sometimes listening involved hearing his anger and allowing him to vent. Other times it involved reassuring him. Yet other times we would just hold each other and cry together. Children have hurts and pain just as we do. Listening provides an open door to their hearts and a window of opportunity for comfort to their souls.

Another principle in helping children through the storms is to be honest about what happened. How much detail should we share when asked questions of them? How much of our pain do we let them see? Honesty with children does not mean we need to air out all the details and dirty laundry of the event. The amount of truth you divulge depends upon your child's age, personality, and maturity. Tell them what they need to know, and take your cues from them. Honesty can be sharing with them what you feel they need to know at the moment and then sharing some information later. Honesty is a very personal judgment call. The grieving process is different for each child. Some will want to know every detail of the tragedy; other children may need to hear a little at a time. Whatever you feel your child can handle, stick with being honest. It's this communication of honesty that will help to provide his or her security.

Another principle for guiding a grieving child is to do something fun! We call them "mommy/daddy days." This time is spent one-on-one with each child doing activities they enjoy doing with us. The recipe for this activity is fun, fun, fun!

All you have to bring to the table is an open heart, to laugh and enjoy your child. For instance, days spent with each child could be going to get breakfast together, going bowling, playing at the park, shopping, catching a movie, getting a manicure and pedicure (Caroline's and my favorite), going to the bookstore (and Matthew's and my favorite), going to GameStop (Philip and Matthew's favorite), going to Moe's (Caroline and Philip's favorite), or any activity the child enjoys. This means, too, that we adults need to be fully engaged in the activity! So, yes, I even got to climb a "mountain" at the park with Matthew and play tag with Caroline on one of our particular special days. As you know, it's not what you do; it's the quality time spent together.

Remember how kids think during times of the storm. Children are learning to be independent and need more reassurance than normal. Discipline your children for defiance, but always remember the child is looking to you for basic validation. Don't get so caught up in the storm that you withhold this. *Apologize for any mistakes you made that contributed to the storm*, but be careful not to withhold what every child needs.

And lastly, the all-time best healer of grief is the power of prayer! Prayer provides healing to the soul and a close relationship with the One who can comfort and heal. It's in these precious moments of prayer with our children that they learn the importance of leaning on the Lord for comfort and strength.

Is Your Name in the Book of Remembrance?

Philip Wilson

You know the world is crazy when the best rapper is a white guy, the best golfer is a black guy, and the tallest guy in the NBA is Chinese.   Chris Rock

A FRIEND ASKED ME IF I ever worried about the future. If so, what did I worry about? I have to confess I do worry. There are times when I am feeling weak and worry about what could happen: What is the next storm brewing for the Wilsons? Is something going to happen to Rhonda? Will Caroline be healed? Will Matthew be okay? Will I have another stroke? Can I rebuild our finances?

I do worry, but not in the same way I once did. I know what it feels like to wake up in the morning feeling one way and go to bed with your world upside down. I don't worry as much about how I am going to handle whatever comes my way during the day.

I have realized there are just times in our lives when we will be "called to suffer" through an unwanted situation. We will be called to glorify God through a storm, and it won't be easy and it won't be fun, but we must accept it.

When Job was pressured to curse God for what had happened to him, he responded in Job 2:1, "Shall we accept good from God, and not trouble?" He had lost everything but managed to remain steadfast through brokenness.

Grief from tough times is managed by pressing on. Just like iron in a forge, we are shaped by pressure and high temperature. Grief is managed by offering more thanks to God than requests of God. Your grief will last the length of time you take to accept your circumstances. It may be intense for the rest of your life, but I promise you that if you meet your challenges by trusting your creator to work it out, you will find your grief is not so intense.

We live life looking forward but we understand life looking backward. To live life forward, you need to trust God will provide what you need in your life. The more we focus on what is wrong in our life, the more our life produces what is wrong. The more we focus on God then the more we see how God provides for our needs.

Why is God silent at times when we need him most? I have no idea. I do know that it has nothing to do with me. It does not have anything to do with how I pray, how often I pray, how often I sin, or if I go to church.

It is not about me!

Your circumstances are not a reflection of how God feels about us. God will never let us suffer without it fitting into His plan for our life, and His plan is for our benefit. He will not let us suffer without us profiting from it. When God is silent, He is not absent from our life, even though it seems He does not care about us. We must trust God even though He does not always do what we expect or want. We trust the great change agent has His hand on our life. Philippians 3:10 says, "I want to know Christ—yes, to know the power of his resurrection and participation in his sufferings, becoming like him in his death."

Paul talks about a thorn in his flesh. We don't know exactly what the thorn was, but Paul asked for it to be removed several times. God said no, that His grace was sufficient for Paul. Grace is the power to continue, to press on and to keep on keeping on. God promises that His strength is enough for us to go through our storms. God chooses to showcase His power in our weakness.

Malachi 3:16 describes a book of remembrance for those who fear God. The type of fear mentioned here is one of reverence or awe. It is not fear that God is going to hurt you. It is like fear we would have for someone in authority, such as a teacher or parents. The passage from Malachi talks about how every time we think about God it is recorded. The book of remembrance stays in front of God as a reminder of who is thinking about Him. It is a reminder to God of people who put Him first in their life: those who recognize we were created by Him and for Him to bring Him glory. Those who remember their suffering have a purpose.

100

Living deeper requires us to seek God for who He is, and not for what He can do for us. We were not created just to make money and die. We must learn how to honor Him in all aspects of our lives, especially the storms. Let's move to the point where we can say the suffering was worth it, because it brought God glory.

I did not enjoy what I went through, but I know my God is the great "I am." I trust him for purpose and direction of my life. We can bloom where we are planted until the Lord moves us. We can stop complaining about our problems. We can do our best every day, and leave the outcomes to God. We can choose to praise Him no matter what that outcome is, even if it is not what we want.

In the beginning of this book, we looked at a passage about Paul and the many troubles he faced. What kept Paul going? What was his motivation to press on? The answer is that Paul was aware of the *presence of God living inside of him.* He trusted God, knowing His grace was sufficient and that God would never leave him or forsake him. God would never allow a storm without providing both the strength to endure it and a purpose for it. If you really believe what Paul said—"all things work together"—how can you not have confidence God is in control?

In our world, we seem to look up to actors and athletes who have unique ability and achieve a high level of financial success. The people I look up to are often not famous or wealthy. I respect people who do not quit; those who have the courage to keep going. Their inner strength comes from God. I respect the single working mom who has to raise and support her children alone; the father ran out, but she is not angry. She just wakes up every morning doing her best for God's glory. I respect parents who watch their child get cancer, yet still look upward in praise. I respect the unemployed worker who thanks God every day for his health and family while pressing on in anticipation of the new job. He knows God has a purpose for him and patiently waits. I respect those who praise God while pressing on, despite their circumstances. The guys in pain who continue to stay in the game—they are hurting but they are still here!

Feeling hopeless? Let God do the impossible through you. Get over the resentment that life is not fair. It is not and never will be. God never promised it would be. We live in a fallen world. Our problem is that we need to change our definition of how God provides. We think providing for us means taking storms away, getting rid of them so we never have to deal with them. God's version of providing is presence— strengthening us by walking beside us (grace).

Think about what presence means to children. When they are hurt or have a nightmare, they want your presence telling them that everything is going to be all right. Your presence provides the child strength. Our confidence in dealing with storms comes from the presence of God, not in understanding why trials are happening to us. If we press on doing what God has asked us to do, everything will turn out according to God's plan for us. His plan is perfect and for our benefit.

In Genesis 50:20, Joseph talks about God's faithfulness, despite all the things that happened to him. "You intended to harm me, but God intended it for good to accomplish what is now being done, the saving of many lives."

I believe when you honor God through your trials, you become a magnet for God's goodness. His blessing just has a way of finding you when you least expect it. Be faithful in the storm. Keep moving forward. This act of faith shows you put God first place in your life. I close with this. The Wilson family did not choose the events described in this book, nor did they deserve them. I did not deserve to be paralyzed by a stroke. My sweet wife did not deserve to be victimized or have to take care of her husband while facing such an unknown future the way she did. She did not deserve to live with me as I dealt with the death of my old life after the stroke. My daughter did not deserve to be electrocuted by the negligence of others. She did not deserve the awful pain of being on fire. She does not deserve to go through life with scars. My son did not deserve to have to deal with what he felt was a loss of his father at age three. He did not deserve to witness his sister on fire. He does not deserve to live his childhood with such uncertainty and lack of security.

The desire of the Wilsons is to take a very private matter of suffering and make it public in the hope that it will change lives and honor God. We did not deserve what happened to us, but we embraced it. We hope to equip others so they too may press on through their own storms and watch the great change agent at work. My prayer for my family is to heal and allow our storms to mold us into warriors for Christ.

In Isaiah 43:1–2 God says: "When you pass through the waters, I will be with you; and when you pass through the rivers, they will not sweep over you. When you walk through the fire, you will not be burned; the flames will not set you ablaze."

We are created by the hand of God with value and purpose. God did not design us for easy life. You are anointed by the creator of the universe for storms. I recently heard a testimony of the popular television minister Joyce Meyer. You may know her story. She was molested and abused by her father during her childhood in terrible ways. In her testimony she stated that she was glad those things had happened to her.

I know that sounds crazy, but I understand what she means. She is where she is today because of her childhood. God brought her thorough the storm and changed her in the process. Now she has a worldwide ministry and helps millions of people.

I can relate to that. It is not that you are happy that bad things happen to you, but when they do, you have a sense of wonder and amazement to see how God will bring you through the pain. I can honestly say my storms were worth it. I believe the storms have helped me be written in the book of remembrance. I believe I am a better father and husband. I think I am actually better in business. Yes, storms changed me and my family for the better. They have given me deeper purpose for my life. I did not enjoy the storms and never want to go through those events again. I am not even sure I could, but now I am where I am because of those storms, and I am glad they happened.

When you feel stuck in a situation that seems it will never change, be patient. God will provide the way. Do not give up! Keep on keeping on. Honor God by doing your best. Be faithful in the wilderness, the promised land is in your future.

In Galatians 6:9 we read, "Let us not become weary in doing good, for at the proper time we will reap a harvest if we do not give up."

We were meant to live life boldly knowing we can handle whatever comes along. Learn to let God take care of your storm and stop trusting your own ability to figure it out. Trust God to make the rest of your life the best part of your life. Stay faithful, God will show up in a way you do not expect and do things you never could imagine. Stop worrying about how your storms will work out.

Consider 1 Corinthians 10:13: "No temptation has overtaken you except what is common to mankind. And God is faithful; he will not let you be tempted beyond what you can bear. But when you are tempted, he will also provide a way out so that you can endure it."

The Greek word for "temptation" can also mean tested. God will never let you be tested beyond what you can bear. Your storms are not a surprise to God. Your hurt is not a surprise to God. You may not feel like you can handle what is in front of you. That is okay. I promise you this: if you will just keep moving forward, God will show up, in His time. Our God is a God of justice and He is a God of love. He will make wrongs right. He is always looking for ways to show His power through your weakness.

Make the decision to keep moving forward despite what you see in front of you. Regardless of your situation, regardless of how unfair it is, regardless of how you feel. Power to press on only comes when we keep moving. It is from the decision to keep moving (faith) that produces power in our lives.

The power comes from the presence of God. Moving forward is an act of faith. We believe God is in control and will use our circumstance to bring Him glory. Faith produces power. Power to live boldly knowing we can handle whatever comes our way. Yes, God is in control and He is the great change agent. Our life is in His hands. We have the confidence to live life boldly knowing we can handle whatever comes along.

Remember, 2 Corinthians 12:9: "But he said to me, 'My grace is sufficient for you, for my power is made perfect in weakness.' Therefore I will boast all the more gladly about my weaknesses, so that Christ's power may rest on me."

Yes, God is in control!

$$\frac{2017}{8}$$
$$2009$$

49164658R00063

Made in the USA
Middletown, DE
07 October 2017